ELECTRIFYING PERFORMER . . .
SHY, SENSITIVE SUPERSTAR . . .

He's America's hottest star of the eighties—exciting singer . . . dramatic songwriter . . . sensational dancer . . . actor of promise.

All through his teen years he was adored, loved, envied, and pursued. But, at twenty-four, Michael Jackson, the man, still remains a mystery.

Now you can step behind the footlights . . . meet Michael's family friends and famous coworkers . . . watch him at play with his unusual pets . . . share his private time . . . enter his secret world of fantasy, magic, and dreams.

You've thrilled to the music. You've seen him in action. But you won't have the whole, fascinating picture until you read . . .

THE MICHAEL JACKSON STORY

THE
MICHAEL JACKSON STORY

Nelson George

A DELL BOOK

Published by
Dell Publishing Co., Inc.
1 Dag Hammarskjold Plaza
New York, New York 10017

Dell ® TM 681510, Dell Publishing Co., Inc.

ISBN: 0-440-15592-4

Printed in the United States of America
First printing—January 1984

Acknowledgments

The material in this book is culled from my interviews with various Jackson family members, their friends, and their business associates over the years; interviews and notes fellow journalists have shared with me; and written accounts of Michael Jackson's rise since 1968.

Thank you, to journalists Vernon Gibbs, Brian Chin, Vince Aletti, Robert Christgau, Joey Berlin, Sam Sutherland, John Shelton Ivany, Paul Grien, Tim White, Gerri Hirshey, and Steve Ivory, who gave freely of their opinions and observations of the Jacksons. Don Cornelius, Lionel Richie, Tom Vickers, Greg Phillinganes, Steve Manning, Shirley Brooks, Freddie Perren, Ed Eckstine, Ndugu Chanceler, Reggie Andrews, James Mtume, Quincy Jones, Adam White, Sheila Eldridge, Irv Lichtman,

Elliott Hubbard, Laverne Perry, and Ken Reynolds were some of the industry figures helpful in writing this book. So was the staff at Harlem's Schomburg Center for Research in Black Culture. Special thanks to my mother, my sister, and my niece Ebony for being sweet. Extra special thanks to my agent Robert Cornfield, Madeleine Morel, Karen Moline, my meticulous and tough editor Gary Luke, and the ultimate "hyphen lady," my business manager "Alex."

Finally, I say thanks to Michael Joe Jackson for music that has thrilled me since we both were kids and for illustrating that there is no substitute for dedication and determination in turning God-given talent into *magic*.

NELSON GEORGE
August 1983, N.Y.C.

TO SHERYL LEE HILLIARD
For the good times

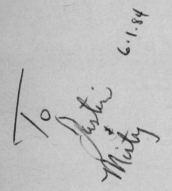

Contents

MAGIC

I wouldn't say I was sexy! But I guess
that's fine if that's what they say. I like
that in concert. That's neat.

—MICHAEL JACKSON, 1983

There is a chill in the air as the sun rises over Encino, California. Outside of Michael Jackson's home young people, male and female, lean against the wall, or sit in cars by the gate, or squat in the bushes. Some wear their obsession on their chests in the form of T-shirts and buttons bearing Michael's likeness. They are a vision of adoration, respect, and love. At times they are persistent.

Katherine Jackson, Michael's mother, has often found them climbing a fence or curled

up asleep in fetal positions on the grounds around the house, their possessions scattered around them on the grass. "They" are so ubiquitous that Michael has developed a sixth sense about their presence; he knows when to roll up his car window at a red light or when not to open a hotel room door. It is a faculty all public figures develop at some point. It comes from the fear of being smothered by a devotion so strong you can't breathe. "You have to be careful because sometimes love can reverse on you," says Michael. "They feel they can't get you, and they'll go to the point of plotting and planning terrible things . . . terrible things to hurt you."

So this morning, as she does occasionally, Katherine walks out to the front gate to talk with them, hoping some good old midwestern common sense and maybe some carfare will send them back to Los Angeles or Bakersfield or even Peoria. "You have no idea of what's really going on in their minds," she has said. Some heed her urging and go. Some stay. Katherine does what she can, yet she knows there will be more tomorrow.

Inside, Michael makes a few phone calls,

getting ready for sessions the next day on The Jacksons' new album and talking with some business advisors about a potential movie deal.

Michael puts down the phone and walks past LaToya's and Janet's rooms, downstairs to a place he usually ignores: the kitchen. He isn't getting anything to eat (the sight of Michael eating is an event so rare that even his brothers are surprised when it occurs) but reaches into the refrigerator, picking out a can of Welch's grape juice. He is a strict vegetarian. After a sip he moves through another room, past his extensive collection of statues (including one striking Cupid-like figure named Michael), and back up to his room. He closes his door and moves over to his bookcase, where numerous books on acting are shelved along with Jehovah's Witnesses' publications which feed his deep spiritual beliefs. Next to it is his stereo, the most prominent object in a room filled with just his bed and a simple desk.

Michael is getting ready to engage in one of his favorite rituals: a Sunday full of long, hard dancing during which he brushes up

on old Jackson Five moves and tries out
new routines with an eye toward the next
tour. "Moving your body is an art," he
contends. "Dancing is really showing your
emotions through bodily movement. It's a
wonderful thing to get on the floor and just
to feel free and do what you want to and just
let it come out. . . . It's escapism, getting
away from everything and just moving the
body and letting all the tension and pain
out."

But first he pulls out an old record. The
gathered fans outside who snap their fingers
to "Beat It" would be surprised to see Michael,
the biggest superstar of the eighties, lying
quietly on his bed as Gordon MacRae thun-
ders through "Oh, What A Beautiful Morning"
from *Oklahoma*. Michael's mind fills with images of the ultimate wide-screen Technicolor
musical featuring all his favorite stars. There
is Fred Astaire and Ginger Rogers. And over
there Judy Garland with Liza. In the background, smiling and looking as pure as a deep
winter's snow, is Julie Andrews. In the middle,
in tux and tails and dark blue glistening shoes,
is Michael, gliding through the middle of a

chorus line, his hair flying all around the set with the biggest, widest smile the world has ever seen on his lips. On the big screen he is commanding, and all the audience can do is watch with wide open eyes and wonder, "What will that boy do next?"

On May 16, 1983, forty-seven million television viewers got the answer to that question. They were watching NBC's *Motown 25*, a tribute to the quarter century of hit recordings from the label. All the great stars to emerge from that once small record company appeared: Diana Ross and the original Supremes, Mary Wells, the Temptations, the Four Tops, Junior Walker, Stevie Wonder, the Commodores, Smokey Robinson, Marvin Gaye, and Martha Reeves. But amid all that talent it was the performance of a twenty-four-year-old showman that most dazzled the crowds.

After a nostalgic medley of Jackson Five hits sung with his brothers, Michael was suddenly alone at center stage. "I have to say, those were the good old days," he said softly. "I love those songs. Those were magic mo-

NELSON GEORGE

ments with all of my brothers, including Jermaine. . . . You know, those were good songs. I like those songs a lot . . . but especially, I like the new songs." The crowd shouted in anticipation. Michael popped on a top hat. The drumbeat opening of "Billie Jean" flowed from the speakers. Now the audience screamed. What followed, said *Rolling Stone* magazine, was "the most electrifying five minutes of the evening. He showed off moves that owed as much to street 'break' dancing as to traditional Motown choreography: stop-on-a-dime spins, some astonishing backward walks." It was *magic*, to invoke one of Michael's favorite terms. "I love to create magic; to put something together that's so unusual, so unexpected, that it blows people's heads off," says Michael of performing. "Something ahead of the times. Five steps ahead of what people are thinking. So people see it and say, 'Whoa, I wasn't expecting that.' . . . When I hit the stage it's all of a sudden a 'magic' from somewhere that comes and the spirit just hits you, and you just lose control of yourself."

Next day the consensus across the nation—

in coffee shops, on street corners, on buses—was that Michael Jackson had come of age.

Of course, those stunning five minutes onstage represented only a single moment of a career that began twenty years ago.

GOIN' BACK TO INDIANA

If I had it to do over again I'd do the same way. . . . I don't want to brag, but looking at the kids, I think I've done a good job. It was hard, but it sure has paid off.

—JOE JACKSON, 1970

When Michael first came to national attention in 1970 he was often compared to Frankie
Lymon, lead singer of the 1950s vocal group
the Teenagers. In 1956, when he was just
thirteen, Lymon enjoyed national hits with
"Why Do Fools Fall In Love" and "I'm Not A
Juvenile Delinquent." Michael had the same
high adolescent voice as Lymon. In fact Michael recorded the Lymon hit "Little Bitty
Pretty One" in 1972.

But here the comparison ends. At the height

of his fame Lymon became addicted to drugs. Because of unscrupulous management Lymon earned little from his hits. At eighteen his career was over. At twenty-five he was dead. Lymon was a victim of the drug abuse and the corruption that have destroyed the lives of so many entertainers. Michael, however, has never fallen prey to drugs, drink, or any of the other vices. The reason can be traced back to his close-knit family. The firm hand of father Joseph and the caressing words of Katherine instilled Michael and his three sisters and five brothers with values that run far deeper than the surface thrills of pop music.

Michael was born on August 19, 1958, and spent his first years in Gary, Indiana—about which he remembers very little today. "I was so small I don't remember," he says. "When I was five I was touring, singing, and dancing. Always gone, always out of school. I just remember little things like the corner store or certain people in the neighborhood. The high school behind [our house] always had a big band with trumpets and trombones and drums coming down the street—I used to love that—like a parade. That's all I remember."

Gary will never be remembered as one of the prettiest cities in the country. Standing on the northern tip of Indiana, just a short ride down Route 80 from Chicago, it is the grim image of inner-city decay. At night the eerie red glow of fire from the city's massive smokestacks dominates the night sky. During the day the sight of old factories and small single-family houses meets the eye. It is a tough working-class city that even back in the 1960s was plagued by high unemployment.

As a result Gary has always had an active street life. Back in the sixties Gary was known to many as "Sin City"; a place where people from Chicago and the rest of Indiana hid from friends and wives. It was this environment that made the owners of the three-bedroom house at 825 Jackson Street, Joe and Katherine Jackson, so careful about rearing their children. At the time they couldn't know they were raising America's first black teen idols. Their main priority was just trying to find enough cash on Joe's salary as a crane operator at U.S. Steel and Katherine's occasional part-time job at Sears to feed and clothe nine kids.

Maureen, their oldest child, was already married and living in Kentucky with her husband Nathanial Brown. The other girls, LaToya and baby Janet, were safely under Katherine's supervision. It was the six boys who worried them: Sigmund Esco a/k/a Jackie, a tall, solidly built teen who showed the promise at both baseball and basketball; Toriano Adaryl a/k/a Tito, a quiet stocky, round-faced youth who resembled a slightly smaller version of father Joe; Jermaine La Jaune, whose long, easy smile and shy eyes made him a favorite of all the neighborhood girls despite his stutter; Marlon David, a dance fanatic who loved learning the latest steps and showing off at parties; Michael Joe, a small impish bundle of energy who loved to laugh and could always be found playing with animals; and little Steven Randall a/k/a Randy, who loved following his brothers around, especially Michael.

Joseph Jackson and Katherine Corse were married in 1949. He was twenty-one. She was eighteen. In attitude they weren't very different from any typical middle American couple. He was the strong-willed provider; she was the family's comforter who both stood behind her husband and guided him at the same time.

To Joe, child rearing required a stern attitude like the one his father had exhibited raising him in Tennessee. "My father was very strict. He was a schoolteacher and he treated me just like the rest of the kids in school. I'm glad that happened. I might not have been able to do the things I've done without a very strict raising." Around the Jackson home he was the disciplinarian. Joe remembered that back home in Tennessee it took hard work to survive. He had found the same true in the "big city" of Gary and didn't want that lesson lost on his children.

Katherine, in contrast to her aggressive and somewhat intimidating husband, is a calm, quiet woman whose strong heart "is the foundation that families are built on," says a family friend. Polio struck her when she was a child, and ever since she has walked with a slight limp. Though Joe was raised as a Lutheran, it was Katherine's faith in the doctrines of the Jehovah's Witnesses that deter-

mined the Jackson family's religious training.
Of the children, Maureen, LaToya, Janet,
and Michael have been the most dedicated.
When they were young, Katherine would take
them to the local Kingdom Hall, the Witnesses
equivalent of church, three times a week.

Jehovah's Witnesses have often been criti-
cized for predicting the end of the world; for
saying that men are superior to women; for
refusing blood transfusions; and other doctrines based on their strict interpretation of
the Bible. But for Michael that early religious
training has had a lasting impact.

The Witnesses' *New World Translation of
the Holy Scriptures* endures as one of his
favorite books. "I believe in the Bible and I
try to follow the Bible," he says. "I don't just
pray at night. I pray at different times during
the day. Whenever I see something beautiful,
I say, 'O God, that's beautiful.' I say little
prayers like that all through the day."

Consequently Michael has little patience
for a completely secular interpretation of the
world. "A lot of people don't believe [there is
a God]. Science is so silly sometimes. The
sun has been up there for ages and ages.

What holds it up? I don't care how many scientific explanations they give me, it ain't deep enough for me." To this day Michael attends a California Kingdom Hall, and although he has one of the world's most recognizable faces he still performs his "door-to-door ministry," selling *Watchtower* and *Alive* from house to house.

While religion became one of Michael's continuing interests, his older brothers found their release in sports, Jackie, Jermaine, Tito, and Marlon—at the urging of their father—participated in all forms of team sports. Jackie was an outstanding high school athlete and won numerous trophies for his aggressive play. In the schoolyard the Jackson boys, particularly Jermaine and Marlon, were smooth and graceful players. Years later, on an international tour, they played and beat a professional basketball team in the Philippines.

Whenever possible Katherine encouraged her children to find entertainment at home. She loved organizing them into groups for the favorite Jackson family card game, tonk, and other indoor games like Scrabble and

Monopoly. Singing was an important part of life at the Jackson house. Katherine's clear soprano led the family through standards like "Cotton Fields" and "You Are My Sunshine." Joe would strum chords on the electric guitar he kept from his days of playing with a dance band called the Falcons in the early 1950s. But the Falcons never graduated beyond Gary and he gave up his dream of a career in music for a nine-to-five gig. So it pleased Joe to hear the harmonies his family's vocals could produce.

Tito was fascinated with Joe's guitar and would play it when his father wasn't home despite the family rule that it was not a toy and strictly "off limits" to the kids. Then one day, as Michael remembers, "My father caught Tito with the guitar and he got so mad 'cause he didn't want anybody to touch his beautiful guitar. It was something he cherished, and he kept out as a memory piece. When he found Tito playing it he whipped him, let him have it. Then he said to Tito, 'Let me see what you can do.' And he meant it. Well, Tito picked up the guitar and started *really* playing. My father was shocked 'cause he saw some special talent there. He was really surprised. He was so happy that his son could do this."

After Tito's display Joe realized that Jackie and Jermaine were also evolving musically and could sing onstage. Jermaine showed promise on bass, too. Initially it was this trio, the Jackson family, who by 1965 had begun occasionally to perform at local talent shows. Marlon was included in the act when he turned six.

Everyone knew it was only a matter of time before Michael would join. Even at two years, his mother says, Michael could imitate Jermaine's voice. In kindergarten he amazed his teachers with a heartfelt version of "Climb Every Mountain." So the older boys didn't complain when Michael, immediately on joining the group, was installed as lead singer. He was five. Jackie recalls that Michael "was so energetic that at five years old, he was like a leader. We saw that. So we said, 'Hey, Michael, you be the lead guy.' The audiences ate it up. The speed was the thing. He would see somebody do something, and he could do it right away."

Now called the Jackson Five at the suggestion of a neighbor, they rehearsed every day
after school, working long hours on dance
steps and vocal harmonies. On Saturday nights
Joe would travel up to Chicago's Regal Theater and watch the vocal groups for steps his
sons might use. The Temptations were a
favorite. In their tight-fitting sharkskin suits,
pointed Italian shoes, and close-cropped hair,
the five "Temps" moved across the stage with
a style both sophisticated and slick; they were
the epitome of the crossover Motown acts
who were as entertaining to South Side black
crowds as to audiences at New York's posh
Copacabana. Joe wanted his sons to be as good
and better.

In the summer heat the boys would work
out. Michael, Marlon, and Jackie would be
up front. On either side stood Jermaine and
Tito on guitars. Other friends and family members contributed on drums and keyboards.
Joe offered critical comments on everything
from Tito's guitar playing to the dance steps
Marlon and Michael made up. Katherine used
her ear to judge their harmonies and her
fingers to sew stage costumes.

"Kids would tease us because we would be rehearsing all the time, even in school," recalls Michael. "There was a big baseball park behind our house and we would hear the roar of the crowd. The kids eating candy and popcorn would come around while we were inside rehearsing. This would get us mad. Rocks would come in through the window, and people would tease us, saying we were wasting our time."

Were Joe and Katherine typical "show business parents" who pushed their kids into fulfilling their own show-biz fantasies? Looking back, Tito answers that "our parents did push us, but it wasn't against our will. We loved music, it was a thrill to be making music at that age that sounded good and that adults seemed to like. The other kids would pass by our house on the way home from school and they'd see us practicing every day. Some of them stopped to listen. Others would make fun. They'd say, 'Look at those Jacksons. They won't get anywhere. They're just doing all that for nothing.' But we kept at it. I think a lot of our success now is because we got started so early."

On this subject Joe comments, "When I saw that they liked it, I kept them at it, I helped them when it got hard for them and when they felt disgusted as kids sometimes do. You know they do like something when they find it easy and get good at it, but when they try to do harder things and they find it more work than they thought, you have to encourage them to get over that hump. . . . When the show business thing became important to them they started to make some money off it. I didn't want to deny them the opportunity to have to have this profession, and I didn't want them to be managed by a stranger who might let them run wild. So I quit my job at the steel mill and gave my time to the show business part of it."

Joe saw that his boys had a chance at the stardom and riches the Falcons had never obtained. "I used to play guitar, with a group. We tried to be professional, but we couldn't get the right type of management, guidance, or contacts, so we never really did anything serious with it."

For Katherine music was, at this point, still a way to keep the boys off the street and the family together. If it turned into a career, well, that was good. The most important thing to Katherine was not the money, but that the music solidified family unity.

Most of the material the Jackson Five performed in the mid-1960s came from Motown acts. The first record Michael ever bought was the "Mickey's Monkey" by the Miracles. When the Jackson Five won their first talent show at Gary's Roosevelt High in 1965 they sang the Temptations' "My Girl" and "Get Ready." Even then Michael had a taste for grittier soul sounds, and at his suggestion Sam and Dave's "You Don't Know Like I Know" and "Hold On, I'm Coming," Lou Rawls's "Tobacco Road"—and anything by James Brown—were added to their repertoire.

In a town where there were few opportunities, many dreamed of success in music as a way to escape Gary. Winning a talent show was a good way to build a reputation. But sweeping contest after contest the Jackson Five quickly became a local legend. Katherine's living room became filled with trophies. Michael was already being called "a thirty-five-year-old midget" by the acts that went up against them in talent competitions.

The Jackson Five established themselves as such a popular local attraction that a small Gary-based label, Steeltown, signed them. The first-ever Jackson Five single was called "I'm A Big Boy Now"; like their early Motown records it was slanted lyrically to take advantage of the group's age.

"Big Boy" was a standard rhythm-and-blues ballad of the mid-sixties that leaned heavily on call-and-response vocals between Michael and his brothers. Michael's voice is surprisingly husky. Apparently he was told to sing in a lower register than normal for the recording. On the "B" side, "You've Changed," Michael sings an undistinctive tune in his natural tenor-soprano range. "Big Boy" was picked up for distribution by Atco, a subsidiary of Atlantic Records, and was a minor midwestern hit.

The "A" side of the Jackson Five's second and last Steeltown single, "We Don't Have To Be Over 21 (To Fall In Love)," is less distinguished and didn't sell. The flip side, "Jam Session," is of more historic interest since it features Michael on congas, Jermaine on bass, Tito on bells, and father Joe himself on electric guitar—his only recorded performance. Overall the Jacksons showed signs of promise on both singles, but they were still rough diamonds.

Despite Steeltown's limited distribution both records generated some airplay in Gary and in the surrounding states. That exposure led to the group's first paid gig, at a Gary nightclub called Mr. Lucky for which Joe Jackson was paid five dollars. But in those early days the Jackson Five were not solely dependent upon what the club owners paid them, since audiences often threw money to them as they performed. "When we sang, people would throw all this money on the floor," Michael recalls. "Tons of dollars, tens, twenties, lots of change. I remember my pockets being so full of money that I couldn't keep my pants up. I'd wear a real tight belt. And I'd buy candy like crazy." Some nights the boys picked up as much as three hundred dollars.

Katherine didn't like letting her sons perform at nightclubs. But the extra income certainly helped, and she was pragmatic enough to concede to her husband's business decisions.

Still, there is no denying that some of those early clubs hardly offered the best atmosphere for young boys. Michael recalls, "When we used to do nightclubs, some of the things I used to see from the stage—you'd probably think it was nothing—but I was around six at the time and this woman, one of the strip-teasers, would take her drawers off and men would come up to her, and they'd start doing . . . Aw, man! She was too funky! Ugh! That to me was awful!"

But Michael wasn't always so shy. When the group would do the Joe Tex hit "Skinny Legs and All" Michael "used to go in the audience and lift all the girl's legs up. God, I'm so embarrassed about that. I would never dream of doing that now."

During 1967 and early 1968 Joe and the boys worked hard to polish their act in preparation for the ultimate challenge for unknown black performers at that time: the amateur-night competition at Harlem's Apollo Theatre. Every Wednesday night the Apollo, known for its raucous audiences, had a backstage filled with untried acts hoping to win the talent show and the prize of a paid engagement there. Notable first-timers who have entered that contest are Ella Fitzgerald, Sarah Vaughan, Billie Holiday, Leslie Uggams, and Joe Tex. Because the Apollo was in New York, the home of the big managers, booking agents, and record companies, a winning performance there was often translated into the start of a successful career.

In the summer of 1968 the Jackson Five were invited to compete. "I remember the night of the show," says Joe. "There was this object just offstage which resembled a tree trunk which was supposed to bring good luck to first-time entertainers if you touched it just before going on. Although the object was onstage behind the curtain it was positioned so that most of the audience could see you when you touched it. I remember the kids touching it before they went on. One thing about the Apollo Theatre, if you weren't good, you might get a few cans or bottles thrown at you. The kids were more afraid of that than anything else. We weren't afraid of losing the contest; we knew we had it. We just wanted the people to like us. They went out there and performed, and won; in fact, we got a

standing ovation. . . . And from that point on
we got invitations to come back to the Apollo
Theatre to perform for money."

By the end of 1968 the group's reputation
was such that, even without a record deal,
the Jackson Five were a popular attraction on
"the chitlin circuit," a network of theaters
and nightclubs around the country that had
supported black performers during the years
when they were barred from white concert
halls. All the boys, Joe, and often Katherine
would pile into a Volkswagen Microbus and
drive east to the Apollo, Philadelphia's Uptown,
and the Howard Theater in Washington,
D.C., or west to Phoenix and Kansas City, to
do as many as seven shows a day and then
return to Gary for school the next day.

On the long rides from Gary to the concert
halls on the East Coast the boys would have
to study. When it got too dark they'd sing the
current rhythm-and-blues hits that they were
performing or the traditional songs their
mother had taught them. Card games went
on all night. Michael refused to play for money,
even if it was just pennies. Occasionally a
sock fight would break out or some other

rowdiness, but Joe would just turn around in the driver's seat, and everything would calm down. On the rides back to Gary, at the end of the evening Joe didn't have to worry. After an initial flurry of talk about how the songs had gone, followed by Joe's often stern critique, the boys would one by one drift off to sleep. They knew if they didn't get any sleep they'd probably go the rest of the day without it because they'd finally reach Gary around four or five in the morning. By six they'd be up getting ready for school. During the day they struggled to stay awake. Joe did the same at work while operating his crane. Later that afternoon rehearsals began again, first led by Katherine and then, after five, by Joe.

For Michael those early road trips were an education in entertaining. "I would sit on stage at shows and watch James Brown and Jackie Wilson perform. I would watch and really feel it, particularly the crowd and the way they reacted. That's what I wanted to do. I felt it so much it seemed like I could just run up there and do what they did. I sat there every day and watched."

Don Cornelius, nationally known for his

syndicated television show *Soul Train*, was a DJ at Chicago's WVON in the late 1960s. He remembers "promoting a show with them at the West Side Theater in Chicago before they had signed with Motown. Even then they were a phenomenal group and sort of the talk of the town. They were in fact so dynamic that many established acts in town did not want to be caught on the same stage with them. At that time Michael was the closest thing to James Brown you could find. Now, they were all fine performers, but to see a seven-year-old with that kind of command was most impressive." Cornelius says that even after the group signed with Motown the stage show wasn't altered significantly, "it was just that the music Motown provided them with was so superb that it changed the ambience of the group."

Freddie Perren, who would later produce the Jackson Five's first singles at Motown, was another appreciative early observer. "I was with Jerry Butler in 1968, and we were playing a club in Chicago. That was Jerry's hometown so he was very popular there. When I saw these little kids opening the show for us

I really felt sorry for them and hoped the crowd would be kind to them. Michael was so little and innocent. You know how a crowd can be. Well, Michael just destroyed the audience. He was amazing, just an amazing performer. Hey, it was very rough trying to come on after that, let me tell you."

Despite Michael's flamboyance onstage, he was still a shy boy. Even though he idolized the black stars he was now seeing on a regular basis—their dressing rooms were just feet from his—Michael rarely introduced himself. When the hydraulically-operated microphone disappeared into the floor at the end of each performance Michael was too shy to ask a stranger where it went. But still curious, he wended his way downstairs, through the dirty basement of the old theater, to find it.

During this period Joe sought out a partner with experience in the entertainment industry to help the Jackson Five secure a contract with a major label. He approached a number of major performers of the era, including Sam Moore of the great soul duo Sam and Dave, with an offer to sell half his management rights to his sons for five hundred dollars. Moore recalls that he passed at the time because he thought the group's kiddie sound didn't have the style of rough, gritty Memphis soul he knew best.

Joe finally found his partner in New York, not backstage at the Apollo, but at the New York office of the musicians' union. He was a young white lawyer named Richard Arons. The offer came after Arons, a musicians' union staffer, was asked to help Joe fill out forms necessary for the Jackson Five to perform at the Apollo. They got along well. Joe asked Arons if he was interested in comanaging the boys. While he was reluctant at first, the answer was a firm yes after he saw them onstage.

Joe's partnership with Arons isn't well known outside the record industry. Joe remained the group's chief spokesman, while Arons used his experience to handle the nuts-and-bolts negotiations for the Jackson Five. It proved to be a partnership that would benefit all concerned for the next ten years.

How the Jackson Five came to Motown's

attention isn't completely clear today. Motown stars Gladys Knight and the Pips had performed with the Jackson Five at the Apollo and the Regal in 1967 and 1968, and say they told Motown about the group. Later Bobby Taylor, lead singer of a minor Motown act called the Vancouvers, played with the Jackson Five at a club in the Midwest and got them an audition with the record label. James Jamerson, bassist on all the immortal "Motown Sound" hits of the 1960s, remembers their appearance with Taylor at Motown's Hitsville studio as rather humorous. "They brought these kids around and said they were the Jackson Five. Well all the musicians started cracking up, because Jackson was a slang expression like 'Jackson Jive,' so here they come the Jackson Five."

The "official" Motown version is that Diana Ross saw the Jackson Five in 1968 at a special celebration called Soul Weekend in Gary sponsored by Mayor Richard Hatcher. Ross and the Supremes, the Vancouvers, and the Jackson Five entertained. For Diana it was love at first sight. "Michael won me over the first moment I saw him," she told *Newsweek* in

1970. "I saw so much of myself as a child in Michael. He was performing all the time. That's the way I was. He could be my son."

Joe Jackson disputes this story. He recalls his first contact with Motown came through Bobby Taylor of the Vancouvers, though "actually Gladys Knight had been talking to me about Motown for a year or so before I'd come in contact with Bobby Taylor. But at that time I was trying to make up my mind. I had sent Motown a few tapes, and I never did get any reaction from the tapes. At the same time Gladys Knight was telling me to go to Motown with her. It took a year to be convinced, and finally Bobby Taylor convinced me. I was supposed to have been going to New York—that's what I was supposed to be going to do, because we were supposed to perform on a television show. Instead of going to New York, I said, 'Hey, we're going to Motown.' We stopped off at Motown and didn't get a chance to go to New York."

Tom Noonan, formerly of Motown and now with *Billboard*, recalls a version of the signing with elements of both stories. He says, "When Richard Hatcher was first running for mayor of Gary back in 1967 he met with Berry Gordy [founder and president of Motown] at his house on the West Coast. (I believe Harry Belafonte hooked them up.) He was asking for support for his election campaign, and Gordy did help him. They were planning a concert fund raiser in Gary, Indiana, and Berry let him have Diana Ross and Bobby Taylor." Joe Jackson apparently had been tight with Hatcher and they were put on as the opening act. "Now, Bobby Taylor had been talking about the Jackson Five before this, but it wasn't until Diana called Berry full of enthusiasm for these kids that Berry got interested. If anybody else had called I don't think it would have happened. Diana is the reason he got excited.

"All the Motown executives and the Jackson Five were flown out to Detroit to a party at Berry's mansion, which was now used just basically for parties. They set up their instruments by the pool house and they just killed us with their energy."

Jackie Jackson remembers "it was the biggest place we'd ever seen. His backyard was like a golf course and he had an indoor pool. He had us entertain at a party and most of the Motown artists were there. That's what really scared us. We were up there doing their songs." Where Jackie recalls being wary of the stars, Michael remembers only the evening's triumph. "We did our show and they loved it. They gave us a standing ovation. Berry Gordy came over, and Diana Ross came over at the end of the show and she kissed each one of us. She said she loved what she saw and wanted to be part of what we do."

After that party Motown flew the Jacksons to Los Angeles, and they didn't return to Gary for two years.

It was a heady time for the family. They were about to join a roster of acts that had been dominating the pop and soul charts for six years, groups that had inspired the boys to sing and perform in the first place. So Joe signed the group to the standard Motown contract of the period. That meant a royalty rate of only 2.7 percent, which at the time wasn't unusual for an unknown group. In addition the contract put all the Jacksons' musical decisions in the hands of Berry Gordy and Motown. This again was normal at the company since few labels have ever had Motown's deep reserves of songwriting and production talent. For the Jacksons, budding young musicians, this would prove to be an increasingly frustrating situation. But that turmoil was well in the future. The group were concentrating on the present and their move from 825 Jackson Street to a new life in the City of Angels.

To understand the world Michael entered at age ten when the Jackson Five joined Motown is essential to understanding him today. Motown was founded in 1959 by Berry Gordy, an aggressive ex-prizefighter and record-store owner turned hustling songwriter. Though he wrote hits for Jackie Wilson and others during the 1950s, Gordy was increasingly frustrated by his inability to receive his proper songwriting royalties and the failure to have his songs recorded as he wished.

As a result he decided to challenge the major New York-based record companies that dominated the music business by trying to compete with them. It was a bold move. There had never been a major record label based in Detroit and never had there been a black-owned record label of any lasting importance. Yet, in a success story of heroic proportions, he built a powerful record company out of a small house in Detroit.

He had two secrets for success. First, he was an extraordinary judge of talent; he found and then cultivated Smokey Robinson, Diana Ross, the Temptations, and Stevie Wonder from street kids into world-class stars. The other secret was his meticulous control of every aspect of the company. At his direction Motown held all songwriting royalties and managed its acts. The "Motown Charm School" took ghetto-bred performers and taught them to dance, talk, and how to handle themselves before any kind of audience. There were even classes on table manners—which silverware to use in what order at formal meals—and how a lady sits in a dress.

By 1968, however, the Motown's control had loosened a bit, since Gordy was increasingly preoccupied with shifting the company's operations to Los Angeles and expanding the business into films. Yet in the Jackson Five he saw an unique opportunity to develop an act that was perfect for tapping the lucrative teen-age market. Motown hadn't had a performer with that kind of appeal since the early 1960s when Stevie Wonder was called "little" and "the twelve-year-old genius." Since then Stevie and Motown's other groups had grown to appeal to older audiences in nightclubs and on television.

So Motown took the Jackson Five's raw talent and "groomed" them as it had all its artists, but in a fresh, "hipper" style suitable for the 1970s. Instead of the tuxedos Motown had given the Temptations, the Jackson Five were outfitted in gaudy psychedelic clothes and love beads. Instead of Marvin Gaye's short, neatly trimmed hair the Jackson Five sported huge round Afros that eventually became their trademark. They worked with professional dance instructors—not to transform the boys into miniature versions of Gladys Knight's Pips, but to enhance their already considerable onstage energy. Even then everyone knew Michael was a spectacular and gifted dancer.

Although Berry Gordy ran a strict company that tended to control even the personal lives of performers, there was a very human side. A familylike closeness developed among company executives, staffers, and artists. So, when the Jacksons moved to Los Angeles, Gordy and Diana Ross spent many informal hours with them just hanging out. While the rest of the family stayed at Gordy's house, Michael was Diana Ross's special assignment. He lived with her for a year and a half, during which time she entertained him, coached him, instructed him in the discipline and tradition of Motown.

In this young boy she saw all of her early ambition and desire. And to Michael, Diana was the epitome of success. The hours they shared together then, and over the next decade, had a profound effect on Michael. When he called her his "mother-lover-friend" he did not exaggerate her importance in his life.

When the Jacksons moved to Los Angeles it was Ross who hosted a private party at the Daisy Club to introduce them to the press and the music business. Their first album was entitled *Diana Ross Presents the Jackson Five* to let everyone know the importance with which Motown viewed this unknown group from Gary.

Another part of the record business that Berry Gordy knew very well was media management. With the Jackson Five there was an image to make and protect. For example there were no unexpected revelations about the boys in their first cover story in the national black weekly *Jet*. The story, in the August 6, 1970, issue, had no quotes from the boys and only a brief one from Joe. Instead, unnamed Motown staffers and spokesmen commented breathlessly, "They are still the thank you, yes ma'am, yes sir type" and "their personal development rivals their professional development." In another instance journalist Ben Fong-Torres was told by Bob Jones, head of Motown publicity, "Just two things you gotta promise me. No questions about drugs or politics. They aren't into that and we'd rather lay off it."

From that time Regina Jones, who published *Soul* magazine, remembers "the Jackson children as some of the best mannered, well behaved I've ever met, in or out of show business. They had been well trained. Had great manners. If anything you sometimes thought they were too nice, that they didn't have enough freedom." But even then she could see that Michael's personality at ten differed from those of his brothers. "We took them out for a photo shoot in a park in L.A., and it wasn't long before they were out there playing basketball. Michael wouldn't play. He preferred to sit there and talk. He'd ask questions about everything. He could be in a crowd at their house with groups of people around and just sit there with his sketch pad drawing. You could see he was a thoughtful, sensitive child."

At Motown release of the Jackson Five's first record was much anticipated. "You were so wowed by their visual act that you knew once they had a record they'd be great live," recalls Noonan. "Motown has always been in the forefront of having acts that were slick on stage. To me these kids were the slickest yet. All we needed was a hit."

Gordy knew the key to breaking the Jackson Five in the marketplace was a good song, one that both exploited Michael's youthful energy and established an identifiable sound for the group. So for much of 1969 Gordy sifted through material looking for the song that would turn the Jackson Five's commercial potential into gold records. It finally walked into his office one day in the form of three unknown songwriters.

THE SOUND OF YOUNG AMERICA

It wasn't just the obvious tricks that got the kids leaping out of their seats, it was the total mood of buoyant pride: we've all arrived, brothers and sisters, and we're all goin' take the world.

—SIMON FRITH, 1975

The walls of Freddie Perren's workroom in his Los Angeles studio are lined with gold and platinum albums. High on one wall is "I Will Survive," recorded by Gloria Gaynor which he produced and cowrote. A few feet away Peaches and Herb's "Reunited" hangs proudly. This old-fashioned ballad, again produced and cowritten by Perren, has become a standard. Gold records by two family acts in the mid-1970s, the Sylvers and Tavares, also hold places of honor. Despite Perren's success with these performers it is the several gold and platinum discs that *don't* bare his name that are his finest achievements.

"I Want You Back," "ABC," "The Love You Save," and "Sugar Daddy"—the first four Jackson Five singles, all number-one pop singles in 1970—were products of Perren's full flowering as a writer-producer. With partners Deke Richards and Fonce Mizell, and the aid of Berry Gordy, Perren got the Jacksons off to a resounding commercial and artistic start—an unprecedented accomplishment in pop music history.

"I Want You Back," released the winter of 1969, is regarded by many as one of the greatest records ever made; the explosion of driving rhythms mated with a strong, insistent melody and what is still one of Michael's richest vocals. "Catalyzed by a red hot performance from ten-year-old Michael," wrote *Rolling Stone*, "the record explodes off the turntable with an intricate Sly influenced arrangement featuring some of the toughest bass, drum, piano, guitar playing on any soul record anywhere."

Perren recalls the heady days that produced

those now classic Jackson Five hits. "The records were made by a team called the The Corporation," says Perren. "The Corporation consisted of Deke Richards, Fonce Mizell, myself, and Berry Gordy, who oversaw the records. Deke had been a staff songwriter-producer at Motown in Los Angeles, and after we had written a few songs together, he worked out a deal for Fonce and me and to join him at Motown. Berry came in later after we had written 'I Want You Back.' he gave us the title The Corporation."

Perren recalls that the original title of the song was "I Want To Be Free" and that they had originally intended to give it to Gladys Knight. "But the track was so good and strong, we decided to try to get Diana Ross, the company's biggest star, to record it. We took it to Berry. We played it, and he liked it. But then he said, 'I signed this group of kids out of Gary, Indiana, and if you rewrite it this would be good for them. Direct it toward kids, so they can identify with it. A Frankie Lymon type thing.' Only then did I find out these were the same kids who had been so hot back in Chicago. So with those boys in mind we rewrote the lyrics and it came out 'I Want You Back.' The Friday evening after we cut the rhythm track, we rehearsed the group at Deke Richards's apartment. They learned the vocal parts quickly and we went into the studio. When we finished, it was great. The performance that the group gave tripped me out and I still think it is one of Michael's greatest performances. We went straight from where we were to another studio where Berry was working. Our chests all stuck out, because we knew this was good.

"He listened to it, turned to us, and said, 'You guys are getting ready to blow a hit' and he proceeded to tell us what was wrong, from the arrangement to the lyrics. That night we were up to one or two in the morning. Michael and Marlon were falling asleep, they were so tired."

Even in those first studio sessions Michael revealed a tenacious spirit and dedicated professionalism. "I would have him do the song and by the time we got to the end, it sounded so good, he had improved the performance so much, that I would have him go back to the beginning. This would go on.

First the beginning was better. Then he'd keep on and the ending was better than the beginning. With every take he got better."

When Motown finally okayed the single's release, even they were amazed at its immediate mass acceptance. The new decade would open with the Jackson Five's "I Want You Back" at number one, well on the way to selling over three million copies.

Noonan remembers, "We gave their records an all-out major push, but they weren't difficult records to break. A major promotional push by a record company still doesn't guarantee a hit. There has to be something in the record and there definitely was in 'I Want You Back' and 'ABC.' " With Michael's high-pitched vocals up front, the Jackson Five created a new genre: *bubble-gum music*. White performers such as David Cassidy, the Partridge Family, the faceless cartoon group the Archies, and the Osmond Brothers followed in the wake created by the Jackson Five's success. None, however, endured. The Osmonds were perhaps the most notable followers, with young Donny in the parallel lead position with Michael.

Motown vice-president Ewart Abner commented at the time, "Imitation is the sincerest form of flattery. We here at Motown are not mad at anybody. We wish them luck, while we go on doing our thing and they go on doing our thing."

After those four initial hits, The Corporation and other Motown producer-writers kept the group near the top of the pop charts with seven other Top 20 pop hits through 1972. ("Mama's Pearl" number two, "Never Can Say Goodbye" number two, "Maybe Tomorrow" number twenty, "Sugar Daddy" number ten in 1971; "Little Bitty Pretty One number thirteen, "Lookin' Through The Windows" number sixteen, "Corner Of The Sky" number eighteen in 1972, plus Michael's first solo hit "Got To Be There" number four in 1971.)

Perren saw signs of Michael's songwriting talent even back then. "I never saw any songs he wrote, but I always knew he could," says Perren. "There was an instrumental hit out, 'Love Is Blue' in about 1970. He came in one day and asked me about this section of the song he found interesting. So I showed it to him on the piano. He couldn't play, but he was able to pick it out with one finger on the piano. He was able to learn this part and would sit there picking it out. There is a certain talent that goes with writing songs and I could see he had it. Motown just didn't encourage it in performers."

The Jackson Five's impact had been so profound that when the group finally cooled off a bit Freddie Perren remembered, "We had been so successful at the start that when some of the other records, like 'Mama's Pearl' and 'Sugar Daddy,' only went gold we felt like were slipping up."

In conjunction with all this fine music Motown was occupied with the task of making Michael, Tito, Jackie, Jermaine, and Marlon the most popular young men in America. Coming on the heels of the 1960's politics of confrontation the Jackson Five were a breath of fresh air. They were cute. They were a wholesome midwestern family—with both parents together and active in molding their children's values.

Because of their clean-cut image and bounding vitality, the Jackson Five emerged as popular television performers. The boys' first television gig was the 1969 Miss Black America Beauty Pageant—before any of their hits had made the charts. But it was their appearance on Ed Sullivan's legendary Sunday-night CBS variety show that launched the Jacksons into the mainstream. Every week the nation's most popular entertainment series showcased a remarkable cross-section of talent and celebrity: from dancing bears, pop stars, and Las Vegas comedians to astronauts and acrobats. Ed Sullivan brought the world to American living rooms.

So, an invitation to perform on the show was both a certification of success and an opportunity to expose the country to the newest pop sound. Elvis did it in the fifties; the Beatles did it in the sixties. The Jackson Five joined that elite cadre of pop stars in 1970. "From Gary, Indiana! . . . Here's the youthful Jackson Five," Sullivan shouted, "opening with a medley of their hits that have sold over a million each, er, each skit . . . hit!" Sullivan may have stumbled on the introduction, but the Jackson Five did not disappoint. The camera cut to them and the crowd began screaming wildly. Moving to the throbbing beat, Tito, Jermaine, Marlon, and Jackie formed a frenetic line as the diminutive twelve-year-old Michael, decked out in a garish vest and bell-bottoms, microphone in hand, delivered a segment of "I Want You Back" before blending into "ABC." He devastated the audience with his dance steps and won every heart with his falsetto.

That performance firmly established them as television material and the Jackson Five became the favorite "special guests" on Johnny Carson's *Tonight Show*, Dick Clark's *American Bandstand*, *Soul Train* (a black version of *American Bandstand*), and ABC's *Hollywood Palace*, on which they appeared with Diana Ross and the Supremes.

The print media loved the Jackson Five, too. All the major national publications, *Look*, *Life*, *Time*, *Newsweek*, *The Saturday Evening Post*, *The New York Times Magazine*, and of course *Rolling Stone*, devoted long features to the Jackson family's amazing rags-to-riches tale. Two new black fan magazines, *Right On!*

and *Soul*, seized upon the Jackson Five as symbols of what young blacks could accomplish through hard work. No issue of *Right On!* was complete without several color pictures of the boys, while *Soul* went so far as to devote entire issues to each group member.

Through press releases and photographs Motown took the boys' individual interests and shaped them into easily identifiable "personalities" whose features all the press disseminated through their coverage. Jackie was the gifted athlete who might have played professional basketball or baseball. Tito was the grease monkey who loved cars and spending time by himself. Marlon was the dancer who spent much of his spare time creating steps for his brothers. Jermaine was the "pretty boy" heart-throb trying to find "the right girl." Michael was the cute little brother who liked to draw and enjoyed being part of a group with his big brothers.

But despite efforts to build up the other brothers and make Michael just a part of the group, it was clear he was the Jackson Five's chief attraction. His sweet, child's voice and dancing—that mix of James Brown, Jackie

Wilson, and his own original twists and turns—
were what drew the crowds.

Michael's charisma was apparent to all who
witnessed their 1971 national tour, shows that
were more than concerts, but "events" that
created a frenzy not seen since the Beatles.
In Milwaukee the Jackson Five drew 115,000—
the largest crowd for any concert in that city's
history. To escape the throng the boys had to
use a heavily guarded police boat to leave the
arena. At New York's Madison Square Garden the concert was sold out two weeks in
advance, which should have warned the arena's
security guards that the crowd would be
excited. Ten minutes into the show, according to one newspaper account, "the barrier
was smashed like so many pieces of kindling
wood before the idol-crazed charge of pre-
teen and teen-aged girls." After order was
restored the Jackson Five returned to finish
the show. Later a Garden official was quoted
as saying the Jackson Five wouldn't return
there "unless the governor promises to bring
out the National Guard."

With success come awards, and the Jackson Five won many. From the record indus-

try came awards from *Billboard* and the National Academy of Recording Arts and Sciences (the Grammy Awards). Black organizations such as the National Urban League and the National Association for the Advancement of Colored People honored them for their music and strong family image. The editors of the teen magazine *Sixteen* gave them a slew of awards.

But for the Jacksons the most important award came on January 31, 1971, when for the first time since they had joined Motown, they returned to Gary. Despite a blizzard and forty-mile-per-hour winds the Jacksons helicoptered onto West Side High School Field and were met by almost a thousand dedicated fans. At Gary City Hall Mayor Richard Hatcher presented them with the key to the city, an award that still has an important place in the Jacksons' home. Surrounded by police and city officials they returned to 825 Jackson Street, where a large WELCOME HOME JACKSON FIVE banner hung from the roof. The house was so jammed that only a few of their old neighbors could enter. People who had never given them a second look peered through the glass at the Jacksons. Next-door neighbor Mrs. Walter Thompson said, "Everybody here is just glad to see them and how they've progressed."

The show Gary saw that night was far different from what they remembered of the Jackson Five. They had their own hits to sing, an expensive stage setup that included over a ton of equipment, and a support crew of twenty-five. At two jam-packed shows sixteen thousand Gary residents came to cheer their favorite sons.

Jackson mania had taken hold. One night one of the Jackson boys woke up at home and saw a girl standing over his bed. Another admirer, claiming Jesus had sent her, sneaked into the house looking for Michael. "We'd be in our class and a bunch of fans would break into the classroom," Michael recalls of life in Los Angeles, "or we'd come out of the school and there'd be a bunch of kids waiting to take pictures and stuff like that. We stayed in that school a week. One week! That was all we could take. The rest was private school with other entertainment kids or stars' kids, where you wouldn't have to be hassled."

*　　*　　*

In those days the Jacksons lived in the Hollywood Hills overlooking Los Angeles near many other celebrities. "Everybody knew where we lived because it was on the Map to the Stars' Homes, and they'd come around with cameras and sleeping bags. They'd jump the fence and sleep in the yard and try to get inside the house. It really got crazy."

If there was any resentment among his brothers about Michael's becoming the center of attention, he says he never felt it. "Each person has a thing that he does," said Michael. "I sing and dance and the other brothers sing and dance, but I sing lead. A lot of interviewers and fans ask the brothers if they ever get jealous because Michael does this or he's out front all the time and they all scream for him a little more. It's a silly question, but it's interesting. When they ask me I just answer that they know what I do. I've been doing this since I was five years old onstage and I feel it's something that God gave me to do. I'm the one who sings lead. They can sing lead but I've been chosen to sing lead on the songs and I'm thankful to be chosen. They kind of understand it, and they accept it because that's what I do."

Given that early stardom it is a wonder Michael didn't become a spoiled show-biz kid. The Jackson family would never have allowed it. The other boys always treated him like "the kid brother," both to help him maintain perspective and to keep him in his place. Moreover, Joe was always there to put down any explosions of ego with stern words and the swing of a thick belt if it became necessary. Even the Jackson Five had to live by family rules. If they failed to do housework or played around at a rehearsal, their allowances for that week was held back. There was a five-minute limit put on all phone calls by family members. "If you can't say what you need to in that time," Joe reasoned, "then you'd better sit down and think about what you're calling about before you use the phone." Michael, as the group's focus and most mischievous member, often received his father's sternest admonitions. As any parent would be, Joe was concerned about how all that attention would affect his son.

Because child stardom is notorious for turning sour, others were also concerned. One of Michael's most vivid memories of the early years is being stopped backstage by Ed Sullivan when they were on his show. The legendary host told him, "Never forget that God gave you this talent." It was both a compliment and a warning. Even today Michael mentions that anecdote in interviews.

In an effort to escape the attention they drew in Los Angeles the Jacksons moved out to the San Fernando Valley and the wealthy suburban community of Encino. During the early 1970s Encino gained a reputation as a comfortable place for celebrities to live. Its resident's included television stars Dennis Weaver, Mike Connors, Dick Van Dyke, and singer Aretha Franklin. The Jacksons purchased a $250,000 estate full of orange trees and surrounded by high walls. There was an extensive closed circuit television system with a camera mounted on a fifteen-foot pole at the front gate and screens in several parts of the house, including the kitchen. The house sat on the left side of the entrance road. Across from it was a full-sized basketball court—the scene of numerous well-organized basketball games—and a large pool. A $25,000 darkroom was installed to accommodate Michael and Marlon's interest in photography. Behind the house was a $100,000 recording studio where the boys wrote and recorded music that they hoped would one day be on their albums.

Ed Eckstine, vice-president of Quincy Jones's Qwest Records and son of jazz singer Billy Eckstine, grew up in Encino and became friendly with the Jacksons. "Several of them went to the Walton School, an alternative education school with five classrooms and a limited enrollment composed mainly of rich kids and show-biz kids. . . . They had Afros like H-bombs in those days and they used to kid me about my curly hair," Eckstine recalls. Eckstine, a sometime bass player, would talk with Jermaine about the instrument and the problems of growing up in the spotlight. From the experience of growing up around his famous father, Eckstine understood the pressure of always being in the public eye. Yet even he was shocked at the lengths to which the Jacksons went to protect themselves from their adoring fans.

Eckstine says, "It was the first time I'd ever heard of hiring fake limos and doubles so they could get out of the concert hall."

Despite the attention Michael was receiving, Eckstine says, he was just a little kid offstage. "He ran around, played with animals, and loved to draw with watercolors. But as soon as he stepped onstage he went from a kid to an adult—just like that. It was an amazing transformation. But just to show you how much of a kid he was, when something about the Mafia came up in conversation, he said, 'If they come after me I'll just hide under my bed and they'll never find me.' "

Once the older Jackson boys, Jackie, Tito, and Jermaine, were given their own cars they hung out in Encino and throughout the Los Angeles area with "the Motown babies," children of Motown performers and executives. Many of these youngsters attended Beverly Hills High. So it wasn't unusual to see the Jackson boys standing by or sitting in cars in front of the school any afternoon, according to Frank Brown, now a journalist, who attended Beverly Hills High at the time. Brown remembers that Jackie met his future wife

Enid there and Jermaine would sit waiting for Berry Gordy's daughter Hazel to leave school. "Neither Jackie nor Jermaine was obnoxious or loud as you might expect from young stars. Tito was more boisterous. He was always walking around in big hats and gangster-styled clothes. They all hung out with Berry Gordy III and Diana's brother Chico Ross, who also went there. Berry III was on the football team with me. When we played, the entire Motown family would come out; the Jacksons, Marvin Gaye, Diana Ross, and Berry himself, sometimes with a crew to film the game. There might be thirty people in the stands and half would be from Motown. . . . They had a tight group. They'd have pool parties together—the boys would even do some of their Jackson Five routines sometimes—and play ball together."

One of the few outsiders to gain entry into the Jacksons' cloistered world was a Harlem high school student named Steve Manning. He'd heard about the Jackson Five's early appearances at the Apollo Theatre and was impressed by the enthusiasm of everyone who'd seen them. When he finally heard their first Motown hits, "I Want You Back" and "ABC," Manning was hooked. Through mutual friends he met the Jackson Five's road manager, Suzanne DePasse. DePasse befriended Manning in 1970 and gave him the unusual job of answering the ever-growing mountain of Jackson Five fan mail generated by their success. "My room at home was covered with stacks of mail," recalls Manning, now a professional publicist. "Aside from just letters they would send toys, rings, candy, all kinds of stuff. A lot of it I would send to children's hospitals in the group's name. A lot was just given away.

"The Jackson Five then were a very timely group for black Americans. It was the time of the Afro and black pride. Never before had black teen-agers had someone to idolize like that. So girls would write in wanting of course to marry them. Guys would write in, 'I Like your Afro. What do you use to keep it up?' The kids identified with them not as stars, but as contemporaries fulfilling their fantasies of stardom."

Even though Manning was answering the Jacksons' mail, getting access to them was still difficult. "I remember the first time they came to New York and played Madison Square Garden I couldn't meet them. But because I answered the letters, Motown did send a certificate naming me a fan club president." Finally, in 1971, when the group was performing at the Philadelphia Spectrum, Joe asked Manning to come down. "We were in communication, but never face to face," says Manning. "I waited in the hotel lobby for them to bring me upstairs and there were hundreds of people, hundreds of girls, lingering there looking for some way up to the group's room. I was nervous, waiting, thinking maybe they might not come get me. Finally one of the road managers, Tony Jones, came downstairs. When I got there my initial reaction was 'Wow, Michael is such a little boy.' He seemed so small. The group had heard about me and were immediately very friendly. I became extremely close to them and Motown didn't like it, since I had, through Suzanne and Joe, broken the inner circle and was in direct communication with them. . . . It was just the Motown way to keep their artists extremely guarded and protected."

Upon his graduation from high school Manning's family sent him to California, where he stayed as the Jacksons' houseguest. "Randy was a little boy then and Janet was about four. I went out to Disneyland with them, had dinner with them. I really didn't realize how big they were and how envied a position I was in being so close to the group. To go from Harlem out to California where they had a pool and a big house was some difference in life-style. It was the same thing for them, moving from Gary, trying to adjust to a whole new world and new life-style."

The boys peppered him with questions about "everyday life." "Michael and the boys had a great fascination with Harlem. They always wanted to know about the blacks there and what went on there. Even though Gary was a tough city it was nothing like Harlem to them. They loved to hear stories about the violence and crazy things that happened there. They would sit there and say, 'Wow.' "

If the Jackson boys were tantalized by Manning's tales of blood and guts, to the outside world they were still the embodiment of sweetness and light. The Jackson Five

Christmas Album gave new meaning to "heart-warming," with Michael's giddy delivery of "I Saw Mommy Kissing Santa Claus" ("I did, I did . . . I did see Mommy kissing Santa Claus") and a sensitive reading of "Christmas Won't Be The Same Again"—all great family fare.

During the summer of 1971 the Jacksons were mass-marketed. They were given their first network television special, *Goin' Back to Indiana*, which aired concurrently with the release of the single of the same title. The comedy and variety show featured Bill Cosby, a pregnant Diana Ross, Tommy Smothers, Bobby Darin and footage of the rousing concert performed back home in Gary. At the same time a Saturday-morning Jackson Five cartoon series debuted, offering the antics of characters that resembled the boys—which did not, however, use their real voices.

In 1972 Motown released a record that accomplished more than any television special or cartoon series. It created a Michael Jackson trademark. "Ben" was the title song to a quirky horror flick of the same name. It stars

Lee Harcourt Montgomery as a young man
who raises rats for the purpose of revenge.
Essentially, "Ben" (the song) celebrates the
friendship between a young man and a particularly intelligent rat. Despite its musical
qualities, it remains a difficult song to enjoy
with a straight face.

Yet Michael, never one to embrace cynicism,
sings it with a conviction and subtlety he'd dem-
onstrate often in later albums. The yearning,
lost quality when he sings phrases like "never
be alone" would be echoed in his later ballad
performances, notably "She's Out Of My Life."
At some points in "Ben," Michael sounds like
his favorite singer Diana Ross, while his feel
for the drama of the lyric suggests another
favorite, Barbra Streisand. These elements,
plus the childlike timbre of his midrange,
made this a quietly stunning performance.
Matching Michael's vocal The Corporation
turned in its most restrained production: the
brush drums, subliminal string arrangement,
and acoustic guitar are perfect. The record
has a melancholy innocence that fits Michael
and to this day makes it a memorable moment in any Jackson concert.

Michael's love affair with rats didn't end in the recording studio. In 1977 Michael told *Crawdaddy* magazine, "I love rats, you know, like in *Ben*. I really do feel like I'm talking to a friend when I play with them. I used to raise them at home. But now I've gotten out of it. 'Cause rats have a real weird thing between themselves. We used to live up high in Beverly Hills where there is a lot of snakes and they came down to check out the rats. I had about thirty of them in a cage outside. Almost got bit by a rattlesnake one day because of the rats. There was a strange mist around, a rainy type of coldness and the snakes started coming out of the ground to get the rats. I guess I got caught in the middle of this.

"Then I came home one night and looked in the cage and the rats had started eating each other. The father was eating the babies. I got sick of looking at it all. I left their cage outside. I didn't realize how cold it was and the rats still alive froze to death." Michael laughed after he told this story.

In 1972 Michael was involved in another film. As often as his schedule permitted he

visited the set of *Lady Sings the Blues*, a
biography of the late jazz vocalist Billie Holiday starring Diana Ross and financed by Berry
Gordy. "On television I never had any real
time to study anything; we just had to do it.
Quick," Michael said. In comparison "with
the movie, you go over the lines over and
over again. That's why it takes so long to film.
It's got to be right." He wandered around the
set wide-eyed at the excitement and detail of
film making. Like Ross and Gordy, he saw it
was the logical extension of live performance.
Television was one thing, but it was in film
that Michael felt one could make the kind of
grand, enduring artistic statement which increasingly shaped his aspirations. But that
would come later.

By 1972 the Jackson Five's popularity
stretched around the world and they embarked
on an international tour to meet millions of
new fans. In Great Britain they appeared at
the Silver Jubilee celebration, giving a command performance for Queen Elizabeth at
King's Hall in Glasgow, Scotland. It was considered a historic event since the Jackson

Five was one of the youngest pop groups ever to perform for English royalty. In Liverpool, the Beatles' hometown, they broke even the Fab Four's attendance record. At a sold-out concert at the London Palladium, Elton John was the opening act.

On the European mainland they sold out concert halls in Italy, Germany, and France. It was on that and subsequent tours that Michael first saw Europe's historic art galleries and museums, which whetted his growing interest in art. Today he comments, "Whenever we go to Paris, I rush to the Louvre. I just never get enough of it! I go to all the museums around the world. I love art."

In Asia huge crowds cheered them in every country. In Japan they played Tokyo's annual music festival at the Imperial Palace as well as concert halls in Osaka and Hiroshima. To relax from their frantic tour schedule the Jackson family went to see the Sidney Poitier film *To Sir with Love* dubbed in Japanese. In Australia representatives of the native Aborigines hosted a special cookout for the Jackson Five, since they viewed the Jacksons as brothers from across the sea. Michael found India of special interest because of its natives' deep sense of religious commitment. He was fascinated that the Hindus "treat a cow as a sacred animal. It's like a God."

But the most memorable excursion of the period for the Jackson five was a ten-day trip in the winter of 1973 to Senegal, West Africa, at the behest of African promoter Mamadu Johnny Seeka. Seeka believed that by exposing American black entertainers to Africa he'd heighten black Americans' interest in their homeland. The group agreed to three shows in the nation's capital, Dakar, not for the money (in fact the Jacksons paid fifteen thousand dollars to have quality light equipment sent over), but for the experience.

All of the boys were very moved by their first trip to Africa. Kwaime Braithwaite, who accompanied the tour as press coordinator and photographer, observed that the "poverty they saw there seemed to really bother them. Gary, Indiana, is not a rich city, but they had never seen people live as they are forced to in Africa."

At Goré Island, where European and American slavetraders held blacks in preparation for embarkation to America, they saw first-hand the cruel and cramped conditions of the cells. "I studied Goré in high school and college" said Jackie, "but I never did know exactly what it was like until I came over here and saw. I never did know the places were that small, or how they captured them and chained them up like that."

For once they could walk down a crowded street and not be greeted with the frenzied hysteria of their American fans. They were free to observe a native culture that had had a direct impact on their music. Michael commented, "I always thought that blacks, as far as artistry, were the most talented race on earth. But when I went to Africa, I was even more convinced. They do incredible things there. They've got the beats and rhythm. I really see where drums come from. . . . I don't want the blacks to ever forget that this is where we come from and where our music comes from. I want us to remember."

Five years later, in 1979, the Jacksons would become involved with Africa again. The band-had been booked to perform in South Africa. At the time, Mamadu Seeka was being treated for terminal cancer in New York. Yet he called Joe to explain the need to boycott South Africa because of its apartheid rules. Even though the contracts had been signed, Joe was convinced to cancel the date. It is an event that garnered a tremendous international respect for the Jacksons.

More and more the question of artistic expression became an issue for Michael and his brothers. The magic days of spontaneous hits were over for the group. The Corporation—at least partially because Gordy was so involved in making and marketing *Lady Sings the Blues*—no longer supplied the group with the quality new material it once had. More profoundly, by the spring of 1973 the formulas that were the backbone of Motown's musical success were rapidly becoming obsolete.

Black music was beginning to open to a fusion of established rhythm and blues and white rock flourishes. It began with Sly Stone's now classic *Stand!* album—black pop music's first major album seller. Motown's success had been built on singles; their albums contained hits plus lots of filler. Jimi Hendrix revitalized guitar as a lead instrument for black musicians on *Band of Gypsies;* Isaac Hayes's lengthy, seductive album cuts and their play on the growing number of black-oriented FM stations marked the end of three-minute restriction on hit singles (the short single was a Motown trademark).

In Philadelphia producer-writers Kenny Gamble and Leon Huff were cross-fertilizing these new elements, plus a touch of upscale sophistication, to mold a new sound—and a new empire based on the Motown concept with success like the O'Jays and Harold Melvin and the Bluenotes. Even within Motown producer Norman Whitfield was acknowledging the change in the air; he was responsible for such tracks as "Papa Was A Rolling Stone" and "Cloud 9" by the Temptations. The historic recording of Marvin Gaye (*What's Going On*) and Stevie Wonder (*Innervisions*) were issued with the Motown logo, but their personal statements marked radical breaks with the Motown formula.

The Jacksons could hardly ignore this period of innovation in black music. Their cute, bubble-gum hits, all mammoth sellers just a few years ago, now seemed old fashioned. The Jackson Five needed a new sound. Night spots called "discos" were appearing on the East Coast where longer cuts were being played. The boys had been writing some songs that broke from the style on which their reputation had been built. However, the Jackson Five's move into this new dance music was to be choreographed, as always, by Motown staffers.

The result was the 1974 hit single "Dancing Machine," the best Jackson Five effort of the period. Supervised by veteran producer Hal Davis and coarranged by the Commodores' producer James Carmichael, it mixed jet-propelled bass and drum tracks, fine ensemble vocals by the Jacksons, and a high-octane Michael lead ("watch her get down, watch her get down") that made for joyous dancing. However, the same enthusiasm wasn't apparent on the other tracks of the album, such as "Get It Together" and "Forever Came Today." "I Am Love" is basically a lengthy instrumental track with cameo appearances by Jermaine and Michael. Today we can see it as an unfortunate harbinger of the kind of high-tech, low-personality music that overran the discos and the airwaves of the mid-1970s.

That summer of 1974 the Jackson Five were booked into Las Vegas's newest, biggest hotel, the MGM Grand, symbolic of their ascension into show business's hierarchy. But they'd be playing this important engagement without the full backing of the Motown machine. Father Joe, for the first time since the group signed with Motown, was fully managing the group. Motown was loosening its hold on its performers' lives as Berry Gordy's business interests were moving beyond the company's record division.

To Joe this was as it should be. Years later he would say, "It was my wife and I who cultivated the boys and refined their talent. Motown put the word out there and took a lot of credit, but it started with the family." The smart money on the strip bet "these bubble-gum babies wouldn't cut it" without Motown's guidance. Steve Manning commented, "Certain individuals, certain parties, looked for the Jacksons to be a huge bomb at the MGM Grand Hotel. They were sent there literally to fall on their faces."

Yet by the end of the engagement the Jackson Five had set an attendance record and received highly favorable reviews. The family just rallied together. Instead of featuring only the boys, the entire clan—sisters Maureen and LaToya, and the kids, Randy and Janet—were incorporated into the act to heighten the Jacksons' family appeal for Vegas. Katherine came up with the idea that the pint-sized Janet and Randy should imitate Sonny and Cher, Mickey and Sylvia ("Love Is Strange"), and even Jeanette MacDonald and Nelson Eddy. Janet displayed a real flair for comedy in a humorous parody of Mae West. Michael devised elaborate choreography to incorporate the additional family members and introduce show-biz gimmicks into the show. *Billboard* magazine noted, "In 1974, they broke the generational barrier with a dazzling show which included their three sisters, and utilized a mix of Jackson hits and standards, tap dancing, and props designed to win the hearts of the older crowd."

Critic Vince Aletti, who saw the same show performed later in New York's Radio City Music Hall, enjoyed the family's show-biz frills, particularly Janet's contribution. "But no matter how much I love the others," he noted, "it is Michael who is the group's aesthetic focus. His stylized show-biz posing (the bends and turns arm outstretched and sweeping the air in front of him; little self-hugs with his head thrown back) is becoming a little disturbing, at moments even grotesque for a boy who's still a very skinny sixteen. But when he isn't being Engelbert Humperdinck, he's supreme and so controlled it's almost frightening. In his motel room, when he tells you he's in eleventh grade, it might seem strange, but its believable. Seeing him onstage, dancing, and striding confidently out to the edge . . . you just know he had to be lying." To this day Joe views those shows as a special achievement, one that demonstrated their versatility and self-sufficiency to the world.

The success of the family show developed in Las Vegas fueled the Jacksons' ambitions. The boys were maturing emotionally as well as musically, and their desire for input into the music they recorded only increased with time. In the studio at their Encino home the Jacksons jammed when they weren't on the road. In hotel rooms and planes they worked on songs. Jackie had taken to leaving a tape recorder by his bed in case any ideas came to him at night. Tito would work out riffs on his guitar. Michael and young Randy, "messing around" on piano, had already come up with a couple of strong songs. They felt ready to try their hand at writing and producing what they performed. But Motown management, in the form of their old road manager Suzanne DePasse, who was now coordinating the label's artists-and-repertoire division, indicated that things would continue as before.

Certainly the general public had no idea of the trouble brewing between the Jackson family and Motown. In fact the relationship appeared stronger than ever after the marriage of Jermaine to Berry Gordy's daughter Hazel in December 1973. She was nineteen. He had just turned twenty. To commemorate the event Berry pulled out all the stops for a wedding whose cost was put at two hundred thousand dollars. Though the wedding was held in sunny Beverly Hills, Berry gave it the theme of "Winter Wonderland." The invitations were made of a silvery metal, as were the napkin rings and special mugs inscribed with Jermaine and Hazel's names. Mountains of artificial snow were poured everywhere; 175 live doves in cages surrounded the main ballroom, seven thousand dollars' worth of pure white camellias decorated the tables; and a white-suited Smokey Robinson sang "The Wedding Song" penned especially for the occasion. The ceremony was held downstairs in a special chapel, while the bulk of the guests watched upstairs on closed circuit television. It was a new-style, old-fashioned Hollywood event, the flamboyance and extravagance of which still lingers in the memories of those who attended. As soon as the bride and groom had been joined, speculation began in the ballroom about Jermaine's being groomed to succeed Berry as Motown's head. To the outside world, the Gordys and the Jacksons—meaning Motown and the Jackson Five—were now linked forever. Or, at least, as long as two show-biz kids could stay together.

There was a sudden divorce, but not the one cynics were expecting.

The Jackson family in 1970. Standing (*left to right*): Jermaine, LaToya, Tito, and Jackie. Bottom (*left to right*): Michael, Randy, Katherine, Joe, Janet, and Marlon. (© *Roland M. Charles*)

In Los Angeles, 1970. (© *Roland M. Charles*)

With friends, 1970. (© *Roland M. Charles*)

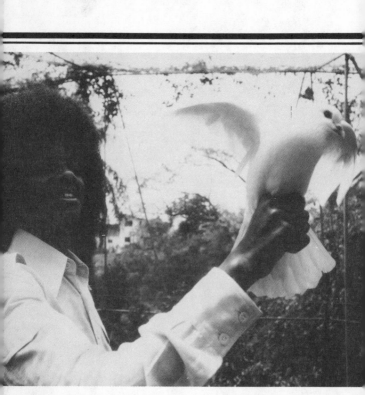

With one of his beloved birds in his private zoo. (© *Fin Costello/ Retna Ltd.*)

At the family's Encino home. (© *Chris Walter/Retna Ltd.*)

Madison Square Garden, 1981. (*Ebet Roberts*)

Madison Square Garden, 1981. (*Ebet Roberts*)

On the set of the "Beat It" video. (*Michael N. Marks*)

With his first girlfriend, Tatum O'Neal, at a Los Angeles party in 1979 hosted by Mayor Tom Bradley in the Jacksons' honor. (*John T. Barr/Gamma-Liaison Agency*)

Center stage at a benefit show for UNICEF in 1980, in his trademark *Off The Wall* tuxedo. (*Stephen Kelly/Gamma-Liaison Agency*)

Receiving the American Music Award for *Off The Wall* in 1981, with Diana Ross. (*World Wide Photos*)

In Los Angeles with Jane Fonda in 1983. (*World Wide Photos*)

The Jacksons' 1981 tour. (*Ebet Roberts*)

Backstage with Olivia Newton-John and *Dreamgirls* star Jennifer Holliday at the opening of that show in Los Angeles, 1983. (*Barry King/Star File*)

Press party for *Thriller*. (© *Chris Walter/Retna Ltd.*)

In Holland. (© *Barry Schultz/Retna Ltd.*)

GOIN' PLACES

You cannot complain about the success you've had in the past where you've had other people write and produce your product. But I guess everyone matures to an age where they in turn can also do the same, and that's the transition that the group is going through right now.

—RON WEISNER
(on the Jacksons in *Billboard*), 1978

JACKSON FIVE LEAVE MOTOWN—SIGN
BIG $$ DEAL WITH EPIC RECORDS,
JERMAINE BREAKS WITH BROTHERS,
FAMILY RIFT CLEAR. . . .

The gradual loss of important acts from Mo-
town's roster (the Temptations, Four Tops,
Gladys Knight and the Pips, the Isley Brothers)
and the decline of others (Martha Reeves,
Junior Walker, the Supremes) had drained
the company of energy and momentum. But
the loss of the Jackson Five in 1976 was seen
by industry insiders as the surprise divorce of
the decade.

The Jackson Five gave the same reasons for
leaving as had the other groups: lack of cre-

ative control and accounting disputes. "Being at a record company is like being at school," Michael said later. "If you're not happy with the principal or the school, you go to another. At Motown we wanted to do our own writing, but that wasn't in our contract and they wouldn't give it to us. We didn't have publishing rights, either, and we had trouble getting a proper accounting of our money. Now we have our own publishing company and we can record anybody we want. Producers were an issue, too. For the *Dancing Machine* album we were forced to use several producers when we only wanted one producer for the entire album, so it would have one sound. Instead we had a bunch of different sounds and it wasn't as good as it could have been."

Another issue was Motown's practice of cutting literally hundreds of songs on an act only to release the very best of them. It was Motown "quality control." The flip side of this approach was that the recording costs—hourly studio rates, engineers' and musicians' fees, equipment rental—all came out of the group's royalties. So before the Jacksons saw a dime on record sales they had to repay all the "hidden" costs. In light of their records' phenomenal sales the Jackson income, while substantial, didn't always match expectations. And since the Jacksons weren't allowed to write any of their own material, they received no songwriting royalties. So this question of creative control also had a deep economic implication.

Motown officials countered that the company had spent considerable time and money in developing the Jackson Five and was just enjoying the return on that investment, and that its contracts weren't completely out of line with industry norms; after all, this control had still made the Jackson family millionaires. In addition Motown complained, with some justification, that Epic, as part of the CBS communications conglomerate, could never treat the Jacksons with the tender loving care to which they were accustomed. "The Jackson Five wouldn't have gotten the treatment they got at Motown anywhere else," claims Tom Noonan. "Not only did they get stage coaching, great production, and strong promotion, but they even lived with Gordy for a while. If they had signed anywhere else someone would have cut a record on them and left them right there in Gary to fend for themselves."

But unlike the departures of the other acts the Jackson Five's exit had another twist: Jermaine's marriage to Hazel Gordy. Jermaine was faced with a very heated dilemma. Should he leave behind Motown and his father-in-law? Staying at Motown meant a full-scale solo career, but also leaving the Jackson Five. "It seemed that the whole world was against me," he recalled. "People didn't seem to realize that I had two families and that whatever I decided to do with my career wouldn't make me love either of them any less. I wasn't choosing between families, I was choosing between record companies."

Finally, after some quite painful soul-searching, the twenty-two-year-old bassist-vocalist decided to stay with Motown. For a time a definite rift was created between Jermaine and his father. "It's my blood that flows through his body, not Gordy's," Joe told reporters. Michael and the others verbalized their support for Jermaine whenever possible, calling it solely "a business decision."

They wanted it made clear that they still loved him and looked forward "to the time we'll work together again."

Jermaine's last performance, a melancholy appearance with the family, was at Las Vegas in the summer of 1975. "Ever since we started singing, Jermaine was in a certain spot near me onstage," said Michael. "All of a sudden he was gone. It felt bare on that side for a long time."

While the family conflict eased with the passing of time, the business battle over the Jacksons' exit raged on into 1980. Motown elected to take the issue to court, seeking $20 million in damages from CBS Records and the Jacksons, and rights to the Jackson Five name. In fact, Motown threatened at one point to put together a new group called the Jackson Five. "We can do anything we want with it," said then Motown vice-chairman Michael Roshkind. "There are/were forty thousand Jacksons running around, and we not only made five of them stars, we put them in their own house, paid for their education— and worked a full year with them before their first record." After three years of court hearings Motown received six hundred thousand dollars in damages and control of the name.

With a new name, The Jacksons, and Randy replacing Jermaine in the lineup, the family looked forward to a greater artistic control of their work. But it quickly became apparent that these hopes would not be immediately realized.

"Let me tell you something," says Manning, "CBS told the Jacksons that they were not talented enough to do their own material. That was one of the main reasons they left Motown—to have the opportunity to branch out. I'm not saying that CBS lied to them, but they certainly didn't give them the opportunity to display their talent. They could have stayed with Motown and been told what to do."

The job of producing the first Epic album, *The Jacksons*, went to Kenny Gamble and Leon Huff, who had pioneered "The Sound of Philadelphia" in the early 1970s with the O'Jays, Harold Melvin and the Bluenotes, and MFSB. On the surface they seemed a good choice to start the next phase of The

Jacksons' career. "Let Me Show You Where To Go," a message song in the recognizable mold of other Gamble and Huff compositions, gave Michael an opportunity to scat a bit. Yet it was, musically, an uneasy relationship. Gamble and Huff's best work had always been with older, gospel-based vocalists such as Teddy Pendergrass of the Bluenotes and Eddie Levert of the O'Jays. Michael's voice was deepening, at age seventeen, but it still had that young and spirited pop quality that was his trademark. Somehow the pieces never quite fit together on their first two albums as The Jacksons.

In retrospect the Jacksons regard these albums as transitional. The Jacksons wrote some songs and received coproduction credit on others, so it proved they could work on equal footing with the finest musicians on the Philadelphia scene.

The quirky, rather uncommercial "Blues Away," written by Michael, marked the blossoming of "Jackson originals" on group and solo albums. The song opens with a bouncy piano riff that recurs throughout the tune and gives the song a vaguely jazzy feeling. Michael did all the backing vocals himself and sings in a breathy tone, techniques he'd use again on solo albums. "Style Of Life," which Michael wrote with Tito, fits right into the bubbling, Latin-influenced groove characteristic of "Philly Sound" recordings. However neither of these songs encouraged Epic Records to feel that the Jacksons could make hit records without outside help.

The Jacksons' own two songs on the next Epic album, *Goin' Places*, issued in 1977, were much more polished and distinctive— although the album did not perform commercially. "Do What You Wanna" is a lively, upbeat song about the need to "keep on striving for your goals." The Jacksons' input into the music was clear, with Tito playing guitar and Randy on congas. A style was beginning to emerge that was quite distinct from the Gamble-and-Huff formula. Even better was "Different Kind Of Lady," a driving dance song built around a looping keyboard and bass groove. Despite the album's failure to garner strong sales, CBS could not dismiss the songwriting and producing progression the Jacksons had made.

Still, in 1976 and 1977, the group maintained a very high profile with numerous television appearances—*American Bandstand, Soul Train, Midnight Special*—and their first series, a summer variety show. The family charm carried such high ratings, that they returned with another series of shows the following winter.

While America was admiring the Jacksons' unity, there were changes occurring at the family's Encino home. The boys had grown into men and were leaving to start their own families. Tito was the first. He married Dee Dee Martes in 1972 and had three children, Toriano, Taryll, and Tito Joe. Jackie and his wife Enid, a Californian he met at Beverly Hills High School, had a son, Sigmund II. Marlon and his wife Carol had two girls, Valencia and Brittany. Randy, like his older brothers, loved sleek, fast cars and was considered a good catch by a number of attractive Los Angeles women. He got his own apartment as soon as he was of age. Still at home were Janet, then appearing on the popular situation comedy *Good Times* and later

Different Strokes; LaToya, then attending college; and Michael. His brothers struck out on their own, but Michael liked the privacy of the family's Encino home.

This is not to say that Michael's personal life was uneventful. Far from it. In 1976 and 1977 Michael had to endure the cruel rumor that he and singer-songwriter Clifton Davis were lovers and that Michael was even undergoing a sex change operation. "I was in a Sears store buying some records while on tour when I first heard about it," Michael related in *Soul* magazine. "This one girl came up to me saying, 'It isn't true, it isn't true!' I said, 'What isn't true?' and she said, 'You're not a girl!' I said, 'What? Where did you read that?' She said, 'It was in *Jet* magazine that you had a sex change.' I felt like I knew who I was at that moment. I told her to tell all her friends that it was just a stupid rumor. The lady at the cash register got so mad at that girl. It was funny. But things like that are a sign of success."

Michael also recalled an evening at Caesars Palace when he was with Diana Ross, and Clifton Davis was accompanied by Leslie

Uggams. "I was holding Diana's hand, and Clifton was holding Leslie's hand. It would have been the perfect shot for a magazine to take the shots and retouch them so that it looked like Clifton and I were holding hands with each other. Do you believe that magazines have been writing that he and I are getting married? I don't believe it!"

Not surprisingly, such malicious gossip is irritating. But, acknowledging it as the unfortunate price of celebrity, Michael said to interviewer Steve Ivory, "I know it's not true, so it doesn't bother me. I'm sure we must have plenty of fans who are gay, and that doesn't bother me in the slightest, but I'm not gay. You can print that. I don't know why people say those things."

Ironically while these rumors were floating around Michael was involved in what *People* magazine described, as his first romantic relationship. The singer had been seen many times in the company of adolescent actress Tatum O'Neal. After the critical acclaim she received acting with her father Ryan in *Paper Moon* she was in the same position as Michael. Everywhere she went Tatum was the center of attraction.

Michael could empathize with the pressures of child stardom and found in her a kindred spirit.

In fact reports reached the press that the relationship had turned torrid at Hugh Hefner's Los Angeles mansion and that they had taken a nude sauna bath together. "Well, I guess I am dating her, in a way," he explained. "I've taken her out a couple of times—or she's taken me out—whatever. I met her sometime back, when Paul McCartney gave a party on the *Queen Mary* boat. She was there and we talked a bit. Two years went by before I saw her again, which was at a club on Sunset Boulevard called the Roxy. We talked and talked and talked. The next day she invited me to join her at Hugh Hefner's house to watch *Roots* on videotape. She got sort of bored, so we went outside and got into the Jacuzzi. We *weren't* naked as people have said. We both had on bathing suits, just enjoying ourselves. And that's it."

In the face of that flurry of speculation about his personal life, Michael could only endeavor to set the record straight. As usual when he was upset Michael turned to music for solace. He was seventeen, about to turn eighteen, the age of passage from high school to college, adolescence to adulthood. Yet he was still faced with the unresolved issue of artistic control and expression. He remarked at the time, "There's a lot of music inside of me that I haven't brought out. We put our hearts into other peoples' songs but they're not the cure, they're not really us."

The Jacksons' writing and producing experiences on the first two Epic albums had told him it was time for The Jacksons to assert themselves. "Different Kind Of Lady" from *Goin' Places* was a big club hit and even Kenny Gamble admitted, "You are good enough to do your own stuff." So Michael, accompanied by Richard Arons and his father, met in New York with CBS Records President Walter Yetnikopf. Michael pleaded with CBS "to give us that chance to prove ourselves. I know my potential and I know what we can do." Yetnikopf agreed that the time had come.

In exchange for producing their next album The Jacksons had to allow two CBS staffers, Bobby Colomby and Mike Atkinson, to serve as executive producers, or overseers. If the group couldn't deliver they would have the authority to come in and finish the album. It was a concession The Jacksons were happy to make, to gain the long-delayed creative control. Colomby, in fact, would make a major contribution to the album by recruiting a promising young keyboardist named Greg Phillinganes to help on arrangements.

"I went out to the house in Encino to work with the guys and was fairly surprised at how much music they had in them," said Phillinganes, who had toured in Stevie Wonder's band. "They were real enthusiastic and excited because this was the first time in their entire careers that they controlled the music. All of them could write, but I thought Michael and Randy were probably the strongest writers in the family."

Working with the Jacksons, Phillinganes grew close to them and they'd share stories about their unusual childhood with him. He recalls, "One time I was sitting in the studio with them talking about how it felt to be traveling through a crowd of screaming people and have hands reaching out and grabbing your hair. Then Michael came over and pulled mine to show how it felt. Well, it hurt; that gave me just a small impression of the kind of world they had to move in."

All the passionate creativity bottled up inside the boys through years of teen stardom revealed itself on *Destiny*, their third album with Epic, issued in 1978. The album—a stunning success—is acknowledged as a coming-of-age performance comparable to Stevie Wonder's *Music of My Mind* and the Beatles' *Revolver*. Unlike their Motown albums *Destiny* had an overriding musical concept built around brotherhood. A peacock drawn on the back of the album cover was selected by Michael as "a symbol of what we are trying to say through our music, and it is summed up by the fact that the peacock is the only bird that integrates all the colors into one. It can only produce this radiance of fire when it is in love. And that is what we are trying to represent through our music. To bring all races together through love. Politics can't save the world, so the music people should at least try. People are brought together through music. With our music, we try to get across the feeling of love and so we relate it through the peacock."

The idea for using a peacock as a symbol of universal love came to Michael after reading a newspaper article about the bird's unique qualities. He knew everyone wouldn't understand or even agree with his approach. For Michael "the significance is important to me and is one of the main reasons I do what I do. If I couldn't bring happiness to people all over the world through my music, I wouldn't do it. I could never just make records for people to buy and just get rich from. That's no good for me. There has to be more than that." As a result the Jacksons' production company is known as Peacock Productions.

Ironically, after all these years of striving for the chance to write their own songs, *Destiny*'s first cut "Blame It On The Boogie" was written by three Europeans. To compound the irony one of those writers was named Michael Jackson. "Boogie" was a light-hearted look at a San Francisco girl who loved dancing so much her boyfriend "don't get no loving and that's no lie." Michael swoops and glides through his vocal with a relaxed confidence while his brothers' smooth, natural harmonies act as a perfect counterpoint. This first single off the album generated the kind of across-the-board radio play the Jacksons hadn't enjoyed since their earliest records.

The albums's strongest cut, "Shake Your Body (Down To The Ground)," was written by Michael and Randy. It earned the coveted platinum disc. Phillinganes lovingly describes it as having "one of the slickest beats and fattest drum sounds you're likely to hear." The effort illustrated the Jacksons' understanding of dance music and studio technology. About three quarters into "Shake" the vocals disappear, as do the guitars, hand percussion, and some other backing instruments. What's left is the synthesizer bass and the drums. The effect was one of the most requested disco singles of 1978. "The long instrumental tag on 'Shake' was totally their idea," says Phillinganes. "I played on the record, but hadn't heard the final version. Michael handed me a copy of the test pressing and with this big smile said, 'Listen to this.' Well, it was hot!"

The last song on the album, "That's What You Get (For Being Polite)," is a moving story of a sensitive young man who remains emotionally unfulfilled. "He cries about you, he cries about me. . . . Don't you know he's scared," Michael sings. The songs can certainly be seen as a precursor to the soul-searching narratives of "Billie Jean" and "Heartbreak Hotel."

The Jacksons were so proud of *Destiny* that they bragged in *Billboard* about its quality. "The past has seen producers producing The Jacksons, writing songs for The Jacksons, which we sang," said Marlon. "We did the best we could, and we were very successful. But this is The Jacksons' music. This is the way we hear music." Referring to the Jacksons' many hours in the family's Encino studio, Tito pointed out, "We've been writing all along, songs that we kept in our own personal bank." The writing on the album was definitely a family affair with all the brothers collaborating on material. Tito added that one of the brothers usually started a song "and later one or more of the others would help finish it."

The same technique was used to produce the album. "When we were mixing the album, a lot of people thought each one of us would have a knob on the board," said Marlon. "But we outslicked all of them. We'd send maybe Tito and Michael in to mix it down, and the rest of us would sit out and wait until they'd get the mix. Then fresh ears would come in and listen to it, because once you keep hearing the song over and over, you lose something. The next song, somebody else would mix down." Summing up *Destiny*, Michael said with well-earned confidence, "I like it, and if I like it, I know they [the public] will. I keep up with the songs and the times. I feel we know what's happening."

Ironically, with all the family's enthusiasm to take their new music on the road, they were forced to cancel seven performances of the 1979 tour. Michael's voice gave out. "My throat was badly infected," he said. "It had blisters on it, and I couldn't talk or sing at all. . . . It was so bad Marlon would hold down certain notes I was supposed to do, and I would stand there pretending I was singing."

*   *   *

With *Destiny* the Jacksons finally had their say. No longer would their creativity be denied. *Destiny* had hits. *Destiny* had feelings and depth. Their father was rightfully pleased. This was the record that all along he had known they had in them.

But now Joe was faced with a different problem. He needed to be sure that Epic Records would give The Jacksons the attention they deserved. To guarantee that kind of support, Joe brought in the management team of Ron Weisner and Freddy DeMann, replacing Richard Arons. DeMann had a long history in record promotion and he had been an executive officer at a number of record companies, including Elektra, and Weisner's background was in management, where he handled the careers of a number of black acts. Their personalities and backgrounds complemented each other and they were starting to build a reputation as shrewd, hard deal-makers. To Joe they sold themselves as just the guys to make CBS sell The Jacksons as hard as they would Billy Joel. His sons had given CBS hot products and

Michael would soon be doing a solo album. If they got the company's full attention there was no question in his mind they'd sell millions again.

THE WIZ

It's a new challenge for me, another world. That's what I love about show business, you never run out of things to do. I always want to go on working all night, work myself to death.

—MICHAEL JACKSON, 1978

Acting had long been one of Michael's goals. He was finally handed a dream-come-true in 1977, when he landed the role of the Scarecrow in the motion picture production of *The Wiz*, an all-black version of *The Wizard Of Oz*. Although the filming required him to move to New York—his first time away from home—it was like visiting old friends: Diana Ross was playing Dorothy, and Berry Gordy was closely involved with the production.

During his time in the Big Apple, Michael

stayed in a two-thousand-dollar-per-month high-rise apartment on Manhattan's posh Sutton Place. His sister LaToya was sent by the family to stay with him. Steve Manning, still on the CBS payroll, acted as Michael's liaison with the press. When not shooting *The Wiz* at the Astoria Studios in Queens or some location around New York, Michael often spent evenings viewing clips of his favorite actors and films, seeking inspiration for his role. Katharine Hepburn and Spencer Tracy films offered examples of charm and relaxation on screen. Fred Astaire's unparalleled dancing grace was a constant source of fascination. Using his video cassette's stop and rewind switches Michael would sit and dissect Astaire's physical attitude.

Later writer Mark Jacobson would observe that "the movie star Michael most closely resembles is Fred Astaire, that paragon of sexual vagueness. Astaire never fit a type, hardly ever played a traditional romantic lead. He created his own niche by the sheer force of his tremendous talent. I mean it wasn't like anyone made up a movie for Fred Astaire and couldn't get him so they got someone else. It was Fred Astaire or no movie. Maybe Michael Jackson is just that good a dancer, that charismatic a performer, that he could do the same."

Michael's favorite screen star is Charlie Chaplin, the sad clown regarded as the greatest comic talent of the silent era. Says Michael, "I just love him to death. The Little Tramp, the whole gear and everything, and his heart— everything he portrayed on the screen was a truism. It was his whole life. He was born in London, and his father died an alcoholic when he was six. His mother was in an insane asylum. He roamed the streets of England, begging, poor, hungry. All this reflects on the screen and that's what I like to do, to bring all those truths out."

Watching Michael in *The Wiz*, Chaplin's influence is quite apparent. Michael's disjointed, flopping movements and retiring, shy characterization were perfect for the role. "I love acting so much," he says. "It's fun, it's just neat to become another thing, another person. Especially when you really believe it and its not like you're acting. I always hated the word 'acting.' Or 'I'm an actor.' It should be more like 'I'm a believer.'"

Unfortunately, the film was a critical and commercial disappointment. The reviewers agreed that Diana Ross, at thirty-four, was simply too old for the part, that the $20 million production was overdone.

The experience, though, was not wasted on Michael. "It took seven months outside in the cold, cold, cold of New York City. It was so cold, some of the dancers had to quit. I enjoyed it to death," he says with characteristic disregard for the discomforting aspects of performing. "It was one of the most wonderful times I've ever had. I went crazy. I learned so much. It was just a wonderful experience. It was a heavy script, real heavy. A lot of people look at it as just a children's story, but it isn't. It's dealing with faith and belief and courage. . . ." In fact, during the shooting Michael had in several instances to be coaxed out of his makeup and costume at the end of the day—so thoroughly did he believe and become the role.

The young actor vehemently defended *The Wiz*: "I watched the old film. I tried not to do it, but then I did watch it on TV a number of times, and sometimes I'd turn the sound off and just watch the moves. I hate to say this, but when you watch the old one you realize that they didn't bring out what should have been brought out. We make the story and the point more recognizable. Like, see, my Scarecrow, I'm full of garbage instead of straw, and all through the flim I don't think I have a brain—but really I do, 'cause I keep pulling these scraps of paper with quotations on them out of my sleeve, that say, 'Confucius say . . .' "

Even with his enthusiasm for acting, Michael says he would never take on a Broadway show. He feels that since it is live, so many great performances are lost. "I feel like I would be giving a whole lot for nothing. I like to capture things and hold them there to share them with the whole world," he said. Yet when a play strikes his fancy, Michael can't get enough of it. He saw *The Wiz* on Broadway innumerable times when he was in New York. And when *Dreamgirls*, the musical based on the Supremes, reached Los Angeles he went to see it three and four times a week. At that show he even became a regular visitor backstage.

*　　*　　*

During those months in New York, Michael did make the whirlwind tour of the favorite haunts of the elite set: dancing with Gloria Vanderbilt at Studio 54; at gallery openings with Andy Warhol; the rock-and-roll scene with Mick Jagger and Keith Richards. While in New York, Michael added two very different female stars to his list of close friends— Stephanie Mills and Liza Minnelli.

Mills was the teen-age star of the Broadway stage production of *The Wiz*. When she sang "Home," the musical's answer to "Somewhere Over The Rainbow," her theatrical delivery thrilled audiences and marked her as a talent to watch. One of her most appreciative fans was Michael. By his own count he saw *The Wiz* eight times, in part because of the upcoming film version but also because he and Stephanie had become friends. Like Michael, and Tatum O'Neal, she was a teen star burdened with adult pressures and popularity.

Those close to the young star say she was quite infatuated with Michael. At cabaret appearances around New York, Stephanie sang "I Wanna Be Where You Are" and used Jacksonesque stage mannerisms. But for Michael she was a good friend, nothing more. Later in her career she often sang a quite passionate version of "He's Out Of My Life," a female version of "She's Out Of My Life," from Michael's *Off the Wall*. Many interpreted it to be a statement of independence from Michael's charms.

Ironically, Michael would also become close to Judy Garland's daughter Liza Minnelli, who, like so many of Michael's friends, had grown up in the glare of publicity that surrounds show business. Coming from the same world of performing, they would "just gossip, gossip, gossip" when they were together. Michael effusively comments on the friendship: "What I like about Liza is that when we get together it's all talk. I show her my favorite steps and she shows me hers. She's a show-stopping performer, too. She has real charisma."

But despite this new life in Manhattan's "fast lane," Michael remained true to the values of the Jackson family. For example Michael claims he's never even experimented with marijuana, saying forcefully, "I've never tired it, and I don't want to try it. I've never tried any of those things. I'm not interested in it. I'm happy the way I am. I don't even like the word 'high.' If I want to feel free with my mind, I'll go walk the beach, read a beautiful book, or write a song. Or spend time with children, which I love to do."

The most productive new association from Michael's *Wiz* experience was meeting Quincy Jones, who was the film's musical director. With over thirty years in the music business Jones had worked with Billie Holiday, Dinah Washington, Frank Sinatra, Count Basie, and Leslie Gore, producing the quintessential teenybopper hit "It's My Party." In the 1960s with the aid of Sidney Poitier, Jones became one of the few blacks to write film soundtracks: *In The Heat of the Night*, *In Cold Blood*, *The Pawnbroker*, and many more. Jones recalls being very impressed with Michael's poignant rendering of "Ben" on an Academy Awards presentation. Watching Michael's work on *The Wiz* set solidified Jones's feeling that here was a major talent. "His performance in *The Wiz* is just mind boggling even for an old-timer, let alone someone who is taking his first shot at film," said Jones.

Michael already had immense respect for

Jones before they met, but, as is everyone who meets him, he was charmed by Jones's warm, loquacious style. Jones took to calling Michael "Smelly," a term Michael uses to mean "funky." By this time Michael was preparing to record his first solo album since leaving Motown, and Jones was the perfect man to produce it. Michael's only instruction to Jones was "to make it sound different from The Jacksons." In that they both succeeded quite magnificently.

OFF THE WALL

I hadn't done a solo album in a long, long time. It was almost as though I was pushed to do this one by some kind of force—really! Right down to the timing. And it all came together nicely.

—MICHAEL JACKSON, 1979

By 1980 it was clear that something was wrong in the record industry. Perhaps it was *Star Wars* and video games; it may have been the sagging economy. In the wake of disco, punk, and new wave, few new musical heroes had emerged. But certainly, fewer and fewer records were being sold.

Into this vacuum stepped Michael Jackson. He had been growing and developing as an entertainer and a musician for years now—but the past decade of success had been with

NELSON GEORGE

the Jackson Five, not as a solo performer.
The most recent album from the group,
Destiny, had sold 1 million copies. So, when
Michael's first solo album—*Off the Wall*—sold
over 7 million copies, it seemed that America
had just found a new superstar.

Off the Wall broke music industry records when it produced four top-ten singles:
Grammy-winner "Don't Stop 'Til You Get
Enough," "Rock With You," "Off The Wall,"
and "She's Out Of My Life." Here was an
album full of fresh and danceable numbers,
eminently hummable tunes, and accessible
lyrics—the essence of pop. Michael had just
succeeded in making his own sound, distinct
from that of The Jacksons.

He had some stellar help along the way.
Songwriting contributions came from Stevie
Wonder, the team of Carole Bayer Sager and
David Foster, and Paul McCartney. The former Beatles' song "Girlfriend," came to Michael quite unexpectedly. At a party that Paul
and his wife Linda were hosting, Michael
recalls just walking in the door when "she
told me that they had a song for me. They just
started singing to me right there on the spot."

But Michael's favorite song on the album was written by the unknown Tom Bahler. It is the romantic ballad "She's Out Of My Life." Producer Quincy Jones remembers that during each take "I'd look up at the end, and Michael would be crying. I said, 'We'll come back in two weeks and do it again, and maybe it won't tear you up so much.' We came back, and he started to get teary . . . so we left it in."

Off the Wall also marked the first full-length collaboration between Michael Jackson and Quincy Jones. It proved to be a marriage of talent and experience. Keyboardist and arranger Greg Phillinganes observed, "Their ideas just blend into each other. You see, Michael is not like a lot of other singers who come around just to add a vocal. Michael is involved in the whole album. 'Q' is basically an overseer who runs the show without really running the show. The icing he adds to the cake can be the difference between a good tune and a great one."

But at the center of it all was the dedicated young musician who sought perfection and originality. The search for a fresh new sound can be an obsessive pursuit. Michael spends hours every day in the studio at home in Encino writing, recording, and experimenting. "He does his homework and rehearses and works hard at home. Most singers want to do everything in the studio. They're lazy," Quincy Jones commented. In fact, Michael often hires musicians to come to the house and jam with him—this is where the ideas originate that eventually become hit records. Says Jones, "When he commits to an idea, he goes all the way with it. . . . It's a long way from idea to execution. Everybody wants to go to heaven and nobody wants to die."

Since his brothers had moved out Michael was writing more by himself and, as *Off the Wall* showed, developing his own separate musical persona. "I try to do it [write] my way," he told Vernon Gibbs. "To copy somebody else's song would make me feel guilty and cheap. It really would. . . . writing lyrics takes me a long time, but writing melodies I love. I make them up all the time. Most of the time I write on drums and piano, though I really wish I could play guitar well."

*　　*　　*

Away from the hectic pace of recording, Michael was afforded an opportunity to reflect on life and art when he visited the film set of *On Golden Pond*. There, on the idyllic lake in New Hampshire, he shared ideas with Jane Fonda, Katharine Hepburn, and the late Henry Fonda. He stayed in a cabin with Jane, whom he'd befriended a year earlier at a Hollywood party. Michael recalls, "We'd just talk, talk, talk about everything. It was the greatest education for me—she'd learn and I'd learn and we'd just play off each other. We talked about all kinds of things, you name it: politics, philosophers, racism, Vietnam, acting, all kinds of things. It was *magic*." Michael tape recorded almost all of those conversations—a way of preserving what is valuable and acknowledging experience he has been denied because of celebrity.

Michael and Jane's father grew close during his stay. The young pop star and elderly acting great found in each other kindred spirits. Jane commented, "Dad was also painfully shy in life, and he really only felt comfortable when he was behind the mask of a character.

He could liberate himself when he was being someone else. That's a lot like Michael. In some ways Michael reminds me of the walking wounded. He's an extremely fragile person. I think that just getting on with life, making contact with people, is hard enough, much less worrying about whither goeth the world."

Katharine Hepburn, the great actress and a private, solitary person, was also charmed by Michael's vulnerability, and became an unofficial acting coach for the budding thespian. In 1981 he visited her East Side Manhattan apartment and was honored to handle some of Spencer Tracy's personal possessions. In September 1981 she returned the favor in a way that surprised the public. For the first time in her life she attended a rock concert, sitting at the side of the stage at Madison Square Garden watching Michael and his brothers perform.

That 1981 tour was the most successful of the Jacksons' career, earning $5.5 million and amazing audiences in thirty-six cities with a deft interweaving of choreography, special effects, 'magic" tricks, and bracing pop music.

Every performance opened with young Randy, miraculously recovered from a devastating auto accident, in medieval armor leading the group to center stage. It had been ten years since the Jackson family burst onto the scene, and much about their act had changed since then. Now there was an elaborate space-age set that Michael had designed. There were now-you-see-them, now-you-don't illusions created by magician Doug Henning. These were the high-tech trappings of the eighties.

Yet at the core of all that activity there was still Michael. Now, at twenty-three, here was a taller, smoother, and more polished performer. There were traces of Diana Ross in his stage patter and in the way he accepted the applause from the audience. With new and refined dance steps, a vitality was evident that rivaled even his idol James Brown. The charisma not only endured, it had expanded.

While all the performances on the 1981 tour generated enthusiastic reviews, two shows at Atlanta's Omni held special meaning for Michael. That growing southern city had suffered a series of unsolved murders of young black children that shocked the nation. At Michael's request most of the proceeds from the Jacksons' two shows there, some $250,000, were earmarked for distribution to Atlanta's poor families. The murders hurt Michael deeply since he maintains an intense identification with children, feeling adults tend to underestimate what children are capable of understanding. "They are more than just children," he has said. "I feel like they are all little geniuses and that they have a secret all their own, a secret they cannot always express. . . . I kind of think they lose it [as they grow older]."

He admires their honesty, noting, "If a kid doesn't like you he tells you, but adults pretend, and they put on phony ways. I wish the world could be full of children." In 1977 Michael predicted that he'd do his part, saying that over the next ten years he planned to have twenty children of his own and "adopt kids, too." Meanwhile, when he is tense or worried, Michael will visit with one of his brothers and play with their children to escape the pressures of adulthood.

The end of the 1981 tour should have been

a time of great pleasure for Michael and his brothers. They got excellent reviews, generated substantial profits, the crowds loved them, and had even aided people in need. But to some degree their accomplishments were overshadowed by rumors that Michael would quit The Jacksons at tour's end. Headlines fed the fire: THE JACKSONS: HAIL, FAREWELL, IS MICHAEL LEAVING THE JACKSONS? JACKSONS APPEAR SET TO SPLIT.

It was true that Michael now had his own career. *Off the Wall* was number one on the charts. He had his own lawyers and accountants. In fact, he had become shrewdly aware of his own business affairs. Once, during a contract negotiation, he surprised Quincy Jones by quoting the royalty rates paid on all of his recordings worldwide. "I didn't know you knew that, Smelly," Jones said.

And Michael is very careful about just how he is presented to the public and the press. The distinctive "Michael Jackson look"—an image separate from the group identity—is the result of assiduous attention to detail. Once, when an unacceptable photo was displayed at a publicity function, Michael—in a rare display of emotion—demanded to know who was at fault.

In fact, there were significant changes in Michael's visual image after the release of *Off the Wall*—the changes that may have resulted from cosmetic surgery. The young man of Negroid features now appears with a slicker, almost European visage. His nose has become long and sleek; his eyes appear as trim ovals that seem wider than before. In the final result, he now favors Diana Ross to a striking degree.

But however mature he became—as a performer or a businessman—the family would endure. Certainly there was no lack of commitment evident on the 1980 group effort, *Triumph*. It is on that album that some of Michael's most innovative and adventurous work appears.

Perhaps the most striking cut is "Heartbreak Hotel," a song about an evil, treacherous way station where faces stare, tear, and glare at the innocent. Though the story line is not completely clear, it seems that ten years ago the protagonist was lured to Heartbreak Hotel and placed in a compromising position.

His love was sent there by the same evil forces and, as was apparently planned, "she thought that I had cheated for another love." On his return visit we meet another lost soul, a man who'd been "here in tears for fifteen years." It reveals a dark side to Michael's vision.

Heightening the impact of this sad tale, Michael filled the song with all of the macabre drama of a story by Edgar Allan Poe. It opens with a mournful string arrangement providing a downbeat prelude to a song that explodes in drums and horns with LaToya Jackson's scream buried somewhere in the mix. Sound effects abound, from drumbeats that sound like cannon fire, to manically laughing voices, to the sound of Michael's antic breathing.

"Can You Feel It" is a song of optimistic inspiration and vision which Michael cowrote with Jackie and for which a full-length rock video was created. The group had dabbled in the form with earlier cuts; this, however, was the first instance with Michael's full creative input. He devised an eight-minute piece, entitled *The Triumph*, depicting The Jacksons as huge, godlike figures hovering over the earth, able to revive a blank-faced mass of people with the golden light that issued from their fingertips. Some critics found the video naive in its sentiment that The Jacksons' music was powerful enough to inspire universal brotherhood.

However, some of the images on the video would seem to spring from the teachings of the Jehovah's Witnesses. They believe that the dead will come back to life and repopulate an earth transformed into an eternal paradise. Indeed, at the end of the video, a peacock—Michael's personal symbol of universal love—appears before the revived population.

But while the world saw a dynamic young performer—effusive and confident on stage—the private Michael was a shy and retiring young man. He was curious about a world he seemed to have experienced so indirectly because of early fame. One person who came to know that offstage persona was Joyce McRae, a former staff member at Joe Jackson Productions.

She was struck by her first conversations with Michael in 1976. He was so persistent in his questions—about everything. What Joyce didn't know then was how that "interview style" would characterize their relationship. "It was embarrassing because I could never evade him, never lie to him. . . . He'd ask me what it felt like to be an only child. He asked me what it was like to be married, if it hurt to get divorced. He asked me if I cried when I got divorced. He wanted to know what it was like to want more children. All these deep intimate things . . . as if he were trying to get an insight and learn more about people. He was really fascinated with the concept of being an only child."

They got to know each other during breaks at rehearsals, backstage at performances— whenever there were spare minutes to talk. Their conversations were private, "not in front of the others," she recalls. "We would usually talk until his bodyguard, Bill Bray, came into the room. And every time, Michael would say, 'Bray, I want to talk. Please let me talk longer,' like a child asking his parents if he could stay up past his bedtime."

One of her favorite memories is of a chance meeting they had at the Los Angeles airport.

"I saw their limo and recognized the chauffeur, Bert Morgan. I was standing there talking to Bert when Bray and Michael came out. We all stood there talking, and all the while I hoped he would volunteer to give me a lift to my house in Encino. But when he didn't, I said, 'I've got to catch the bus to the cabstand.' They pulled off in the limo. I waved good-bye, and they honked. Then all of a sudden I heard someone yell, 'Joyce! Joyce!' and an arm sticks up from the car. The next thing, Michael—not Bray or the chauffer—is running from the limo—diagonally across the traffic—to come and get me.

"I had all this luggage. He kept saying 'Give it to me, I'll take it.' He insisted on pulling the cart back in front of the cars, making like a traffic patrolman! That's the *real* Michael Jackson. When he realized I was still standing there, he didn't care where I was going. He was going to make sure I got there safely."

THRILLER

At twenty-four, Michael Jackson has one foot planted firmly on either side of the eighties. His childhood hits are golden oldies, and his boyhood idols have become his peers. . . . If a jittery record industry dared wager, the smart money would be on Michael Jackson.

—GERRI HIRSHEY, 1983

The winter of 1982–1983 was a busy time for the Jackson clan. Marlon produced veteran soul singer Betty Wright, and she enjoyed a hit chart single with the reggae-flavored "She's Older Now." Janet Jackson was a surprise hit with her debut album, making her black music's 1983 rookie of the year. Janet's album contained two popular singles, "Young Love" and "Say You Do," the latter a good-natured imitation of Michael's "Don't Stop 'Til You Get Enough." LaToya, now a lean young

woman, was recording her third album. Her
first two records had not made the charts, but
with Janet's recent success Joe urged her to
try again.

Jermaine, in what would be his last Motown
album, turned in the best work of his career.
Let Me Tickle Your Fancy showed the considerable influence of Stevie Wonder in his writing and arranging (Stevie wrote, produced, and
sang on Jermaine's 1980 top-ten single "Let's
Get Serious"), but done with a polish and
intelligence that displayed Jermaine's musical
maturation. The title song, a catchy new
wave-funk tune with Devo members Pud and
Spud on robotic backing vocals, was a major
black hit. At the time of its release no one
knew of his dissatisfaction with the label. With
the concurrence of wife and manager Hazel,
he felt that Motown hadn't generated the
sales his music deserved. As a result they
asked for Jermaine's release from his Motown
contract and received it. Father-in-law Berry
Gordy issued a statement that the split "was
not only amiable, but wrapped in love," which
despite its graciousness must have hurt.

There was another surprising split in the

Jackson clan. Quietly, divorce proceedings were started by Katherine in late 1982—after having raised one of the most prominent families in America. The action received little press coverage.

In the midst of all this Jackson activity, however, it was still Michael who managed to dominate the news. His first project was a complete renovation, under his direction, of the Encino home. While it was still considered the center of the Jackson clan, Michael's taste and money decided its new shape, representing an unspoken acknowledgment of his special place in the world and in the family.

"I've always wanted to do this for my mother," Michael has said. "She loves homes and everything, and I do things by feeling and force. I don't feel that it's time for me to move away yet. There are so many things I want to do just staying here. If I moved out now, I'd die of loneliness. Most people who move out go to discos every night. Tey party every night. They invite friends over and I don't do any of those things. I would really die of loneliness."

It wasn't surprising to Michael's associates

that his inspiration for renovating the house was to please his mother. While father Joe has been in the public eye as a consequence of running his sons' careers, it was Katherine Jackson who exercised the strongest influence on Michael's personal development. "The softness and humbleness you find in Michael comes directly from her," says Steve Manning. Says family friend and business associate Shirley Brooks, "She is deeply involved in her religious beliefs and Michael is as well. It is part of what gives Michael his moral foundation. Together they go to the huge yearly Jehovah's Witnesses' assembly at Dodger Stadium." Along with Maureen, Michael is the only one of the Jackson children baptized as a Jehovah's Witness; their relationship is a close one, and he has remained near her side.

A private art gallery is being installed in which pictures from friend Andy Warhol will be prominently displayed. Michael also had a large room set aside to recreate the pirates of the Caribbean ride at his beloved Disneyland. There will be buccaneers, guns, cannons, and tropical scenery; moreover he hopes to have dummies installed that will talk back to him—

all constructed with the aid of Disney engineers. In fact, for a time he was going to Disneyland almost every weekend. To Michael, mannequins are almost ideal playmates, since he can be around them with no threat to his safety. As he told *Rolling Stone*, "I'm putting all this stuff in, so I wouldn't have to go out there."

In the back Michael has his own private zoo housing two fawns (one named Mr. Tibbs), a llama named Louis, several exotic birds (macaws and cockatoos are his favorites), and his eight-foot-long boa constrictor, Muscles. Michael possesses an acute awareness of animals and manifests an intense love for them. In one instance, a photo session in 1983, a makeup artist walked by a cage containing one of his huge birds. She flinched as it squawked and bit a large piece of wood in its cage. Michael sensed her fear. He held her by the arm and made her get as close to the cage as she could. The closer she moved the farther back the bird moved. "You see, the bird is as afraid of you as you are of it," he gently explained.

When *Rolling Stone* reporter Gerri Hirshey

interviewed Michael, she was introduced to his pet boa constrictor in the same way. He let Muscles crawl toward her. She was startled and frightened, but Michael was in control of the situation. "Snakes are very misunderstood," he said, handling his favorite reptile as if it were a puppy. Fear of animals, he feels is what makes them dangerous.

On the musical front Michael continued to branch out as a songwriter. On one transatlantic flight he penned a new song for his former mentor, Diana Ross. The song, "Muscles," was tailor made for Diana, with steamy and suggestive lyrics that took full advantage of her dramatic capabilities. In a brooding tone she pleads for a beautiful male body "to hold on to."

While "Muscles" climbed the charts, listeners were surprised to find that it was written by Michael Jackson. These were the most overtly sexual lyrics he'd ever released. Once again speculation occurred among energetic imaginations that this was a covert admission of sexual preference on Michael's part. Of course, such theories tended to ignore the countless other male songwriters who generate works for female singers. They also ignored the coincidence that Michael's pet boa constrictor is named "Muscles."

Close friend and business associate Shirley Brooks comments, "He doesn't and won't make public statements about his sex life, because, he believes—and he is right—that it is none of anyone else's business. . . . I never let anybody say anything about his sex life in my presence. Michael and I had a long conversation about it, and he just felt that anytime you're in the public eye and don't talk to the press, they tend to make up these rumors to fill their pages. He just thinks time reveals the truth."

Meanwhile, Michael had been spending time with Paul McCartney. Together, both at Paul's Scottish estate and at Michael's house in California, they celebrated their mutual interest in viewing cartoons and Fred Astaire films. The two also emerged as bountiful musical collaborators. They cut two tracks for Paul's forthcoming album: "Say, Say, Say" and "The Man." And, from two men who so love animation, came the very playful song

"The Girl Is Mine," destined for the top of the charts.

That year Michael worked with another of his highly creative friends—film director Steven Spielberg. Quincy Jones had introduced them during the filming of *E.T. The Extra-terrestrial*, and they became fast friends. The idea of turning the *E.T.* story into a children's album was discussed, and the trio decided to collaborate on it following the film's opening. By the time they began work in the fall of 1982, *E.T.* had become so much more than just a film with appeal to children. Michael observed quite succinctly, "Who Doesn't want to fly with some magic creature from outer space and be friends with him? Steven went straight to the heart."

To Spielberg, Michael was perfect for the recording, since "Michael is one of the last living innocents who is in complete control of his life. I've never seen anybody like Michael. He is an emotional star child." The famed director in fact told Michael, "If E.T. didn't come to Elliott, he would have come to your house."

For the children's recording Spielberg put

the story into narrative form, while Jones condensed sounds from the film's soundtrack and John Williams's score to fit the double album. The entire package included the two records, a booklet featuring stills and dialogue from the film, and a poster of Michael and E.T. together. Unfortunately, it was pulled off the market right after release.

Michael's record label, Epic, and the *E.T. Songbook*'s distributor, MCA, suddenly found that they had a marketing problem. Epic was about to release Michael's second, much anticipated solo album *Thriller* and decided to sue MCA to stop distribution of the *E.T. Songbook*. Epic's original request for a temporary restraining order was turned down, but in November 1982 the New York Supreme Court prohibited MCA from selling *The Songbook*. The record immediately became a collector's item, selling for as much as three hundred dollars to hard-core Jacksonphiles and *E.T.* addicts.

But for the time being films and lawsuits were all forgotten as *Thriller* reached the stores. It contained "The Girl Is Mine," which had already reached number two on the charts. But that song provided no inkling of the album's intensity and range. While *Off the Wall* certified Michael as a major solo artist, *Thriller* reached farther and claimed for him the mantle of the most exciting and daring talent of the 1980s.

Thriller was so rich that it displayed Michael's diverse musical personality. The least surprising, yet still pleasing, aspect of the album were songs written by either Rod Temperton ("The Lady In My Life," "Baby Be Mine,") and one Quincy Jones–James Ingram collaboration, "PYT (Pretty Young Thing)." These are solid pop numbers with snappy rhythm tracks and bright, immaculate arrangements.

The title cut, another Temperton tune, could have been written by Michael when he was in the same playful mood that produced "Muscles" and "The Girl Is Mine." It certainly corresponds with his fascination with *magic*. The song chronicles a night of viewing some particularly gruesome horror movies with a lady friend. Spiced with creaky doors and howling voices, "Thriller" climaxes with a campy horror rap by Vincent Price.

Michael's sensitivity and his subtle sexuality have rarely had a better vehicle than "Human Nature," written by John Bettis and Toto member Steve Porcaro (Toto also plays on the record). The music is light, lilting, and quietly haunting, not unlike Michael's speaking voice. The lyric is concise, conversational ("See that girl/She knows I'm watching/She likes the way I stare"), and Michael rolls the words sweetly through his mouth. The tension between the sensual and the innocent comes through clearly.

However, the case for *Thriller*'s greatness ultimately rests with three uptempo songs written and coproduced by Michael: "Billie Jean," "Beat It," and "Wanna Be Startin' Something." Where Michael's songs for *Off the Wall* were happy, these songs cry out for the listener to pull the lyric sheet to understand their mysterious, tortured imagery. These songs burn with insights into Michael's mind. Principle among them is his downright nasty feeling toward people whose tongues, to paraphrase "Startin' Something," become razors.

The evil woman of "Heartbreak Hotel" has

returned in the form of a beautiful, treacherous woman named Billie Jean. In "Startin' Something" she spreads lies and uses her body as a weapon to upset Michael's "baby" and cause her pain. In the song named after this bad lady, "Billie Jean," she again torments him, accusing Michael of fathering her son. In both songs Michael talks of being observed, talked about, and desired. In "Billie Jean" he remembers his mother's advice to be careful whom you love, because it is so easy for lies to be construed as the truth. A fear of the outside world and what people wish to do to him has never been more evident than in "Startin' Something," in which he compares himself to a buffet and a "vegetable" that "they" are eating. Reinforcing that feeling on "Beat It" he notes that, given a chance, "they" will attack you physically and mentally, and still justify their actions (a reference to fans' grabbing and tearing at his clothes).

Children play a prominent role in "Startin' Something" and "Billie Jean," but not as the objects of joy that Michael describes in interviews. The little boy in "Billie Jean" is the result of a now regretted affair. In the future he'd "think twice" about any other such flirtation. In "Startin' Something" he bluntly states one shouldn't have a baby if one can't feed it, a pragmatic and unromantic view of sex. All are comments that can be traced back to the Jehovah's Witnesses' stern admonitions against premarital sex.

Of course strong feelings, even those expressed by a star as well known as Michael, mean nothing without music of equal strength. The rhythms of "Startin' Something" are as complex as "Don't Stop," yet more ominous because of the lyrics. The highlight is a Latin percussion break at the end of the song. The backbeat on "Billie Jean" is a rather sinister shuffle built around three synthesizers, an electric bass, a drum machine, and the skills of drummer Ndugu Chanceler.

Chanceler recalls that "Michael always knew how he wanted to sound. There was originally just a drum machine track on it. I came in and cut a live drum track over the overdub, so that at times during the record there is just me and then the two together." The subtle shifts to a live drum and the combined percussion sound add extra kick to the chorus.

It is little touches such as these, the details that Michael and Quincy love, that distinguish number-one songs from others.

Of the three songs, "Beat It" would have the most far-reaching impact in the music industry. It managed to break the barrier that has kept music by black performers off "album-oriented rock" radio. An element of that success can be traced back to Michael's friendship with actress Valerie Bertinelli. She is married to heavy-metal guitarist Eddie Van Halen, and Michael convinced him to overdub a solo on the song. The unexpected joining of the prince of black pop and the virtuoso of heavy metal was a smart move. "Beat It" was suddenly played across the board on rock stations that seldom featured black artists.

However, the stories of "Billie Jean" and "Beat It" didn't end on record. Michael's ongoing interest in integrating film, dance, and music came into play. The many conversations with Paul McCartney about the making of *A Hard Day's Night* and *Help!*, the countless hours spent in screening rooms analyzing great performances, were all called upon in videos of each. Both illuminate Michael's musical vision. On *Beat It*, for example, Michael detailed his ideas for translating the song in a series of lengthy phone calls to director Bob Giraldi. Then, with *Dreamgirls* choreographer Michael Peters, he blocked out the steps and dance sequences. And when the shooting was done, Michael was there in the editing room.

"Billie Jean" makes an oblique translation from audio to video. The Steve Barron–directed piece is less about paternity charges leveled by a scheming woman against Michael than about the violation of privacy he has suffered and the magical evasive ability he possesses.

Tom Carson's description of the video in *The Village Voice* evokes all of its impressionistic power: "On a rainy, empty stylized city street, a private eye tails a figure [Jackson], whose otherworldly aura is signaled by a human light-show: everything he touches briefly glows an eerie, lovely white. When the detective comes upon Jackson in front of a store every camera in the window goes off, but their pictures only show the private eye reaching for empty air. Finally, we see the reason for the pursuit: Jackson climbs a rickety set of stairs outside a hotel, and comes to a room where he looks down on a woman asleep in bed. He climbs in beside her, but when the detective outside tries to photograph them, the sheet glows and gently collapses where Jackson was lying, and policemen come to take his bewildered tormentor away. As they leave the street, a set of flagstones on the sidewalk gleams in rapid sequence: Jackson, invisibly taking his leave."

Some viewers complained that the images in the sixty-thousand-dollar video had nothing to do with the lyric. In a literal sense they don't. But the song was about public embarrassment, and the pursuer is clearly attempting to capture Michael off guard. But Michael is not another exploitable victim. Michael's powers, as the scene in the bedroom indicates, make his inner life immune to prying eyes and flashing cameras. It all becomes a figment of the detective's (and our) prurient curiosity about his private life. The use of white light as an indication of the presence of *magic* refers back to *The Triumph* video, which in turn was influenced by Spielberg's *Close Encounters of the Third Kind*.

Where "Billie Jean" was influenced subtly by science fiction and fantasy, the $150,000 Bob Giraldi-directed *Beat It* borrowed heavily from tough urban street flicks (e.g., *The Warriors, Escape from New York*) and Michael's favorite musical, *West Side Story*. Unlike most videos it opens with live sound as two gang members leave a grimy East Los Angeles diner on the way to a huge rumble. As the rocking rhythms of "Beat It" kick in, members of the rival gangs gather from doorways, poolrooms, street corners, and even from the sewers. Meanwhile back in his small bedroom our skinny hero lies on his bed looking rather weak.

That is until he dons his red leather jacket, leaps into the hallway, and starts gyrating his stick-figure body. Following the gang members' trail from coffee shop to poolroom to warehouse, he grows in stature. But how will Michael subdue his wild bunch of street kids primed for violence? Simply by dancing. His appearance turns the gang's choreography of violence into a Broadway production-number of ensemble twist and turns. Michael's presence turns hate into love just like *magic*.

Two actual rival gangs were used in the video—with professional dancers. Both had violent histories, yet they were quite friendly to each other and Michael during the shooting, talking with him on the set and bringing presents to his trailer. He took pictures with these street toughs, autographed pictures for their parents, and even kissed their girl friends.

Shirley Brooks remembers one incident on the *Beat It* set that she says "will stay with me forever." In the crowd of onlookers at the shooting was a crippled girl who had come down for the once-in-a-lifetime chance to see Michael up close. "Michael was walking by and everybody was reaching out to him," says Brooks. "She managed to touch him, but he kept walking, trying to avoid the crowd. He went to his trailer. A bit later an aide came out of the trailer and brought the girl to Michael. The two of them sat alone talking for a long time. She had a Jackson Five photo album and he autographed all the pictures. You have never seen anybody so happy as that girl."

By 1983 Michael was everywhere. He was everywhere. *Rolling Stone* conferred perhaps the highest symbol of mass musical success when his picture appeared on their cover. Michael also made the covers of *Newsweek*, Andy Warhol's trendy *Interview*, *Us*, and the hard-rock magazine *Creem*. His stunning performance on the Motown television special just put a cap on the year's achievements. And it was only May.

Just as "Beat It" cracked the rock radio color barrier, *Billie Jean* and *Beat It* videos garnered considerable play on the Music Television (MTV) cable network. MTV had previously held that its audience was only interested in rock or new music videos, and that almost no black performers fit that category. Michael changed all that. After adding Michael's work, Prince, Nile Rodgers, Sylvester, and Bob Marley were among the black artists to receive MTV exposure.

But behind the scenes, a battle was raging over control of Michael's future. The co-management agreement between Joe Jackson and the team of Ron Weisner and Freddy DeMann was due for renewal in March of 1983, and it had become apparent that the

relationship had deteriorated to acrimony. Four
months later, in a bitter exchange in the pages
of *Billboard*, Weisner and DeMann confirmed
the rumors. "There's no great love between
us, and it's no great secret," said Weisner.
They indicated that they anticipated continuing the relationship with Michael—without
Joe's involvement. DeMann went so far as to
say, "We don't have a good relationship with
him, but I don't think he enjoys a good relationship with anyone whose skin is not black."

Joe responded by saying, "There are a lot
of leeches trying to break up the group. . . .
A lot of people are whispering in Michael's
ear. But we know who they are. They're only
in it for the money. I was there before it
started, and I'll be there after it ends."

Joe explained that he had brought in Weisner
and DeMann in 1978 "because there was a
time when I felt I needed white input in
dealing with the corporate structure at CBS
and thought they'd be able to help."

Upon learning of that statement, Michael
contacted *Billboard* and responded: "I don't
know what would make him say something
like that. To hear him talk like that turns my

stomach. I don't know where he gets that from."

Then in a prepared statement, he added: "I happen to be color-blind. I don't hire color; I hire competence. The individual can be of my organization, and I have the final word on every decision. Racism is not my motto. One day I strongly expect every color to live as one family."

Michael did not sign a new contract with Weisner and DeMann. Many were surprised by this unprecedented public display of bitterness. In the end Weisner and DeMann took out a full page ad in the back of *Billboard* that thanked Epic Records for its support during the years they had worked with Michael and The Jacksons. In the next issue of *Billboard* appeared a two-page color photograph of Michael from the *Thriller* album cover, which reported the fact that Michael had sold over ten million copies of this album and that he was the world's number-one artist.

The battle over Michael's management was not just about who would benefit from his recent success, but who would guide his future direction. These are high stakes, for it is apparent that in the entertainment world today there is no star with a brighter future.

Already on the drawing board is The Jacksons' next album, part of which has been written and produced by the Grammy Award–winning band Toto. Independently, Michael has been occupied in a number of diverse projects: he has written a new song with Paul Anka that Johnny Mathis will record; he will contribute new compositions to an album Quincy Jones is producing of duets between Frank Sinatra and Lena Horne; for Barbra Streisand he will write and produce her new album; and he will record a duet with Freddy Mercury of the rock band Queen. Such a hectic agenda suggests Michael's varied interests and goes a long way toward explaining his wide appeal. Such versatility is less a calculated attempt at mass stardom, than a reflection of his idiosyncratic personal tastes. For example, when asked this summer to compile a list of his ten favorite summer songs, along with a number of other celebrities, Michael responded with the most eclectic listing. As expected there was some great black dance music (the S.O.S. Band's "Take Your Time,"

Sly and the Family Stone's "Hot Fun In The Summertime") and some Motown (the Four Tops' "Baby, I Need Your Loving"), but those unfamiliar with his passion for film musicals were surprised at his selection of songs from *Oklahoma* (Gordon MacRae singing "Oh, What A Beautiful Morning") and *The Sound of Music* (Julie Andrews singing "My Favorite Things"). That he cited the Paul McCartney-penned Beatles' song about loneliness "The Fool On The Hill" wasn't unexpected, since its gentle melody and odd little lyric wasn't far removed from some of Michael's own compositions. Yet the majority of Michael's selections were from performers who specialize in soft, mellow music: Seals and Crofts ("Summer Breeze," "Hummingbird"), John Denver ("Sunshine On My Shoulder") and the Sandpipers ("Come Saturday Morning").

As Michael's list suggests he understands the taste of folks raised on rock and those whose taste predates that music, something few of today's pop stars do, His worldwide sales are a reflection of his ability to reach young and old, black and white. *Thriller* is destined to be the biggest-selling solo album in record history, eloquent testimony to Michael's natural universality.

Despite his prowess as a record seller it is clear both from his public statements and video performances that Michael sees film acting as an integral part of his future. As early as 1971 film companies approached the Jackson Five about shooting a remake of the Beatles' *Help!*, because of the parallels between Beatlemania and Jacksonmania. However both the Jacksons and Motown declined the offers. Following *The Wiz*, Michael was offered the title role in a film biography of the great black dancer and movie star Bill "Bojangles" Robinson and a major role in a proposed film version of *A Chorus Line*. Again he declined. Instead, he studied acting with Jane Fonda and Katharine Hepburn. With that experience behind him, Michael is poised for the big screen.

The questions now are, When will he make his next film? What will it be? *Godfather* director Francis Ford Coppola has, at the suggestion of Jane Fonda, asked Michael about starring in a updated interpretation of the children's classic *Peter Pan*. According to James

Mtume, a record producer who recently visited the Encino estate, when asked about it Michael said, "I've already played the Scarecrow. If I play Peter Pan, the next thing you know they'll be offering me Pinocchio." A more likely possibility is the oft-discussed collaboration among Michael, Steven Spielberg, and Quincy Jones. All three have mentioned their real desire to work on a film together, but scheduling has so far prevented them from starting. However, recent reports say that even while shooting the sequel to *Raiders of the Lost Ark* in Egypt, Spielberg was working on a script for Michael.

Will Michael join his heroes Charlie Chaplin and Fred Astaire as a major film star? Will he continue to record regularly and set new standards for creativity and commercial success? The options are his. But all his friends, from Diana Ross to Jane Fonda to Steven Spielberg to Paul McCartney, would probably agree with Quincy Jones when he says, "Michael Jackson is going to be the biggest star of the 1980s . . . and the 1990s."

As for Michael himself, he simply feels, "My real goal is to fulfill God's purpose. I didn't choose to sing or dance. But that's my role and I want to do it better than anybody else."

Across the street from the Pasadena Civic Auditorium, the stars and special guests of Motown gathered in a huge split-level mall following the television taping. On the main floor, at long tables, sat Berry Gordy, Smokey Robinson, the Four Tops, Stevie Wonder, Marvin Gaye, and other performers. They were accompanied by friends and family. Upstairs overlooking the floor the cameras of *Entertainment Tonight* vied for space along the railing with photographers from *Rolling Stone*, *Jet*, and *The Los Angeles Times*. The scene might have been a stiff and proper affair to celebrate Motown's twenty-fifth anniversary.

Happily, it wasn't. Despite their tailored tuxedos and elaborate gowns, the stars of Motown had not gathered to be gazed upon, but rather to party. "I haven't seen so much hard-core boogeying since my last house party," said one member of the Four Tops. People were dancing on tables and drinking Dom

Pérignon as if it were Budweiser. Old friends embraced and cried at every table. Marvin Gaye was dancing with one woman and then suddenly with five. Over in another corner some were singing old Motown songs in perfect harmony, while the DJ blasted new Motown music by Rick James.

Then, high-pitched screams could be heard from outside. The doors opened and there was a harsh glare from a flurry of photographers' strobe lights. Those who were still sitting stood up to see. There, caught in the white light of film cameras, surrounded by four bodyguards and his entire family, Michael Jackson entered the room. He still had on the Navy admiral's jacket from the performance, and worn blue jeans. Michael had hardly dressed for the occasion. The five hundred in attendance hardly noticed. In that room filled with the most prominent stars, the most influential businessmen—the history of Motown—everyone was dazzled by his presence. With almost every eye on him and the long entourage behind him, Michael toured the party, basking in the adoration of his peers and elders.

No star in Motown's constellation shone as brightly as Michael did that night. But in 1983 he was back for one night only. Now, he was his own man making his own music his own way. That "Billie Jean" was the only non-Motown song performed on the show was no accident. In a graphic display of his independence, Michael had demanded that he be allowed to perform the song—or he wouldn't appear at all. He would acknowledge his heritage *and* his future.

He shook hands and chatted at the party, showing no signs of the shyness that sometimes affects him. Michael was the conquering hero come back to show how strong he'd grown. Speaking for everyone in the room, and for the millions awed by his five minutes onstage, one Motown veteran enthused, "The boy is bad, bad, bad, and I still don't think he's as good as he's gonna be. You know what I mean?"

On this night everyone knew. The only question in their minds, one they considered with extreme pleasure, was what would Michael do next? To that question Michael just smiled.

Appendix

*Discography of Albums by Michael Jackson,
The Jackson Five, The Jacksons, and
Other Family Members*

MICHAEL JACKSON

Got to Be There (1972)
Forever Michael (1975)
The Best of Michael Jackson (1975)

APPENDIX

One Day In Your Life (1978)
Off the Wall (1979)
Thriller (1982)

THE JACKSON FIVE

Diana Ross Presents The Jackson Five (a/k/a I
Want You Back) (1969)
ABC (1970)
Third Album (1970)
Christmas Album (1970)
Maybe Tomorrow (1971)
Jackson 5 Greatest Hits (1972)
Lookin' Through the Windows (1972)
Get It Together (1973)
Dancing Machine (1974)
Joyful Jukebox Music (1975)
The Jackson Five Anthology Album (1977)

THE JACKSONS

The Jacksons (1976)
Goin' Places (1977)
Destiny (1978)
Triumph (1981)
Live (1982)

APPENDIX

JERMAINE JACKSON

Jermaine (1973)
Come into My Life (1973)
My Name Is Jermaine (1976)
Feel the Fire (1977)
Frontiers (1978)
Jermaine (1980)
Let's Get Serious (1980)
I Like Your Style (1981)
Let Me Tickle Your Fancy (1982)

JACKIE JACKSON

Jackie Jackson (1973)

JANET JACKSON

Janet Jackson (1982)

LATOYA JACKSON

LaToya Jackson (1981)

Number-One Records Sung by Michael Jackson

I Want You Back (1969) with the Jackson Five
ABC (1970) with the Jackson Five
The Love You Save (1970) with
the Jackson Five
I'll Be There (1970) with the Jackson Five
Mama's Pearl (1971) with the Jackson Five
Got To Be There (1971) solo
Ben (1972) solo
Don't Stop 'Til You Get Enough (1979) solo
Rock With You (1979) solo
Billie Jean (1983) solo
Beat It (1983) solo

(A duet with Paul McCartney, "The Girl Is
Mine," peaked at number two in 1982)

Michael Jackson's Favorite Books
*(A list given to the Young Adult Services of
the Chicago Public Library in 1979.)*

The Greatest Salesman in the World,
by Og Mandino

APPENDIX

The Gift of Acabar, by Og Mandino
Jonathan Livingston Seagull, by Richard Bach
The Old Man and the Sea,
by Ernest Hemingway
The Red Balloon, by Albert Lamorisse
Rip Van Winkle, by Washington Irving
"The Verger," by Somerset Maugham
(short story)
The Complete Works of O. Henry,
by O. Henry
Abraham Lincoln, by Carl Sandburg

*A Selected Discography of Jackson
Five, The Jacksons, and Michael Jackson Singles*
*("B" sides of singles are listed that generated
considerable airplay or sales on their own. All
the important Motown singles mentioned here
can be found on the* Anthology *album.)*

STEELTOWN

Big Boy
b/w You've Changed
We Don't Have To Be Over 21
b/w Jam Session

MOTOWN

I Want You Back
b/w Who's Loving You
ABC
The Love You Save
b/w Found That Girl
I'll Be There
b/w One More Chance
Santa Claus Is Comin' To Town
b/w Christmas Won't Be The Same This Year
Mama's Pearl
b/w Darling Dear
Never Can Say Goodbye
b/w She's Good
Maybe Tomorrow
Got To Be There
Rockin' Robin
Little Bitty Pretty One
I Wanna Be Where You Are
Lookin' Through The Windows
Ben
Corner Of The Sky
With A Child's Heart
Hallelujah Day

APPENDIX

Get It Together
Touch
Dancing Machine
Whatever You Got I Want
I Am Love (Parts I and II)
Take Me Back
Just A Little Bit Of You
Dear Michael
Forever Came Today

MCA

Ease On Down The Road (with Diana Ross)

EPIC

Enjoy Yourself
Show You The Way To Go
Goin' Places
Find Me A Girl
How Can I Be Sure
Blame It On The Boogie
You Can't Win
Shake Your Body
Lovely One

Heartbreak Hotel
Can You Feel It
Don't Stop ('Til You Get Enough)
Rock With Me
She's Out Of My Life
Off The Wall
The Girl Is Mine (with Paul McCartney)
Billie Jean
Wanna Be Startin' Something
Human Nature

VIDEOS

Blame It On The Boogie (1978) Jacksons
Don't Stop 'Til You Get Enough (1979)
Michael Jackson
Rock With Me (1979) Michael Jackson
The Triumph (1980) Jacksons
Billie Jean (1983) Michael Jackson
Beat It (1983) Michael Jackson

MICHAEL JACKSON'S TEN FAVORITE VOCALISTS

Diana Ross
Stevie Wonder

Barbra Streisand
Jermaine Jackson
Jackie Wilson
Aretha Franklin
Paul McCartney
Sam Cooke
Slim Whitman
Otis Redding

(From Dave Marsh and Kevin Stein's *The Book of Rock Lists*. New York: Dell, 1981

Gold and Platinum Records

MICHAEL JACKSON

Off the Wall—gold and platinum
Thriller—gold and platinum

JACKSONS

Jacksons—gold
Destiny—gold and platinum

Triumph—gold and platinum

(Sales for these records were audited and certified by the Record Industry Association of America. When the Jackson Five were on Motown the company didn't allow the RIAA to look at their books, so none of the Jackson Five's Motown hits were officially certified gold or platinum. Gold records have to sell five hundred thousand copies and platinum one million.)

Film Scores

Jackson Five appear on the soundtrack of the documentary *Save the Children* (1972).

Michael Jackson sings the title song to *Ben* (1972).

Michael Jackson plays the Scarecrow in *The Wiz* and sings on the soundtrack album.

Awards

National Association for the Advancement of Colored People's Image Award for Best Singing Group (1970)

Sixteen magazine's Gold Star Award as Best Group of the Year and for Best Single of the Year, "I'll Be There" (1970)

National Association of Recording Arts and Sciences Award to Jackson Five for recording Best Pop Song of the Year, "ABC" (1971)

Billboard magazine named Michael Jackson Top Singles Artist and Top Male Vocalist (1980)

National Academy of Recording Arts and Sciences Awards Michael Jackson's "Don't Stop 'Til You Get Enough" as Top Rhythm and Blues Single of the Year (1980)